T0158341

The Northwest Ordinance

Essays on Its Formulation, Provisions, and Legacy

Edited by
Frederick D. Williams

Michigan State University Press
1989

Printed in the United States of America

All Michigan State University Press books are produced on paper which meets
the requirements of American National Standard for Information Scienced—
Permanence of paper for printed materials ANSI 239.4-1984

Michigan State University Press
East Lansing, Michigan 48823-5202

Library of Congress Cataloging-in-Publication Data

The Northwest Ordinance.

  Bibliography: p.
  Inlcudes index.
  1. United States. Ordinance of 1787.   2. Northwest,
Old—History—1775–1865.   I. Williams, Frederick D.
E309.N68   1988   977'.02   88-42857
ISBN 0-87013-262-8

Contents

Acknowledgments

PROFESSORS DAVID T. BAILEY, HARRY J. BROWN, Gordon T. Stewart, and the late Stephen Botein of Michigan State University, and Professor Gerald Moran of the University of Michigan, Dearborn, helped plan and organize the conference of 3–4 May 1987 at which these studies were presented. Carol J. Blum of the Vernon R. Alden Library, Ohio University, prepared a display of documents and obtained a grant from the National Endowment for the Humanities which made possible the two presentations on education in the Old Northwest. Kathy Kissman, Assistant Director of the Michigan State University Alumni Association, supervised most of the promotional activity. Steven Mattson, a graduate student in history, helped with many conference details and researched much of the bibliography for this volume. The contributions of these colleagues and friends, and the financial support of the National Endowment for the Humanities, the Michigan Council for the Humanities, the Provost's Office and several colleges and departments of Michigan State University is gratefully acknowledged.

This publication was made possible by a grant from the National Endowment for the Humanities.

Introduction

ALTHOUGH THE BICENTENNIAL OF THE UNITED
States Constitution received great attention, 1987 was
also the bicentennial of the Northwest Ordinance, one
of the most important laws in the nation's history. The
Congress of the Confederation, meeting in New York,
approved the Ordinance on 13 July 1787, even as the
delegates to the Philadelphia Convention drafted the
Constitution. For many reasons, some less obvious than
others, both documents merit commemorative activities
aimed at enhancing popular understanding of their origin, provisions, and historical significance.

Adoption of the Northwest Ordinance ended a long
and sometimes acrimonious debate over the question of
how to organize and govern the western territories of the
United States. Through the early 1780s Congress considered a number of proposals for a territorial government and in 1784 a congressional committee, chaired by
Thomas Jefferson, reported a plan that combined old
and new ideas. At first Jefferson's Ordinance of 1784
appeared to be generally acceptable, but its revolutionary provisions aroused strong opposition from Eastern
conservatives and it never went into effect. The following year, however, Congress passed the Ordinance of
1785 authorizing the survey and sale of all government-
owned lands. Execution of that legislation required the
removal of Indians from the Ohio country where the
surveys were to commence. At best, removal was a

wretched operation. To make matters worse, the commissioners assigned to that job used bribery and coercion to get Indian approval of treaties ceding huge tracts
of land to the United States. Angry Indians quickly
denied the validity of those treaties. But the frontiers-
men, believing that the cessions of Indian lands opened
the door to settlement, rushed into the territory. Their
invasion fomented Indian attacks which drew more and
more American troops into the area. By late 1786 a
peaceful solution of differences appeared to be out of
reach.

Those developments punctuated the need for a government for the territory north of the Ohio River. The
Northwest Ordinance fulfilled that need. That document followed the general design and incorporated the
liberal principles of Jefferson's Ordinance of 1784, but
its authorship continues to be a controversial subject. It
was certainly the work of many people, including dis-
honest land speculators who schemed secretly to obtain
for themselves and their associates, among whom were
influential businessmen, members of Congress and
other government officials, millions of acres of land at
pennies per acre. Fortunately, land profiteering was not
the sole concern of those responsible for the Northwest
Ordinance. High-minded leaders viewed the territory
of the United States as a colonial possession entitled to a
colonial government acceptable to the settlers. Fresh in
many minds was Britain's inequitable colonial system
and the revolution it had fomented. Independent, free-
dom-loving settlers who prized local self-government
would not tolerate illiberal treatment. They too would
revolt! At the same time the concerns and political
power of Eastern conservatives could not be ignored.
The divergent views of East and West had to be compromised in a document designed to preserve and facilitate
the development of the country.

As an instrument for achieving those goals the
Northwest Ordinance proved to be remarkable legislation. It guaranteed inhabitants a number of important

rights, including religious freedom, trial by jury, the writ of habeas corpus, the rights and privileges of common law, and protection of private contracts. Those guarantees attracted hordes of settlers and strengthened the movement that resulted in the adoption of the first ten amendments to the Constitution. A provision excluding slavery during the territorial period set an example and perpetuated an attitude that contributed to the ultimate extinction of the institution. Furthermore, each of the five states organized under the Northwest Ordinance fought for the Union in the Civil War, a conflict that became a crusade against slavery. On the other hand, the Ordinance had a reverse effect on freedom for the Indians, who, outnumbered and divided, fought a losing battle to save their lands and way of life.

The fame of the Northwest Ordinance rests primarily on the revolutionary colonial system it inaugurated. Instead of relegating the territories to interminable colonial dependency, the Ordinance established a political process that enabled them to gain statehood and enter the Union as the equals of the original states. Instead of provoking frontier discontent that could have resulted in revolution and disunion, the Ordinance appeased restless settlers, instigated a westward migration, promoted unity, and facilitated growth of the country. Indeed, every state created from United States territories entered the Union in compliance with the machinery it prescribed.

"We are accustomed," declared Daniel Webster in 1830, "to praise the law-givers of antiquity; . . . but I doubt whether one single law of any law-giver, ancient or modern, has produced effects of more distinct, marked, and lasting character than the Ordinance of 1787." Although some may find fault with that statement, presumably everyone can agree that the Northwest Ordinance occupies a prominent place in American history and deserves commemoration.

As 1987 approached elaborate plans were being laid for celebrating the Constitution's 200th birthday, but little was being done on behalf of the Northwest Ordinance. Unwilling to have what one historian termed "the other bicentennial"[1] pass unnoticed, administrators and faculty members of universities in states organized under the Northwest Ordinance decided to commemorate that document. Leadership for the undertaking was provided by Frank B. Jones, Executive Secretary of the Indiana University Alumni Association, who served as project chairperson. The History Department and Alumni Association of each participating university organized and conducted their own commemorative activities. One facet of those activities was an on-campus conference featuring historians who specialize in the period of the Confederation and Constitution.

The Conference at Michigan State University brought together six historians, five of whose essays appear in this volume.[2] The conference focused on "securing and peopling the Old Northwest," and "education in the Old Northwest." A much-discussed topic was the ambiguity of the Ordinance, the theme of Professor Jack N. Rakove's keynote address.

Rakove introduces his study of Congress' "ambiguous achievement" with a brief discussion of the conflicting views of Bernard Bailyn, who has praised the Ordinance, and Gary Nash, who has advanced harsh criticism of the document. Rakove then undertakes to balance the good and the bad by viewing inherent ambiguities of the Ordinance from three perspectives: (1) How and why the organization of the Northwest Territory became a social issue, the answer to which requires understanding a complex mix of noble aspirations, the greed of special-interest groups, ethnic problems, financial difficulties, and practical political problems. Each had to be dealt with effectively in order to complete the struggle for independence. (2) The critically important role of the Philadelphia Convention in drafting a Constitution that gave the new government full authority to develop an effective territorial policy. (3) The legacy of the Ordinance for Native Americans, the harsh treatment of whom was the antithesis of the sentiments expressed in Article III of the Ordinance. Although Rakove conceded that the process of westward expansion was destined to continue had the Ordinance never been adopted, he suggests that the most important and probably the most tragic consequences of the document were a solution of the frontier problem that served well the interests of the United States, and the gross injustices it produced for Native Americans in the Old Northwest.

Professor Gordon Stewart's subject is "The Northwest Ordinance and the Balance of Power in North America." He contends that the debate over the Ordinance must be viewed in a tripartite context: (1) the Old Northwest as "a critical area strategically"; (2) the new republic's "difficult struggle for survival"; and (3) the allegiance of settlers "caught between American and British spheres of influence." American leaders, he declares, feared a British conspiracy "to break the western territories away from the fragile union of eastern states." Refusing either to abandon the Northwest Territory or to postpone a decision on its future, they developed a territorial policy that won the allegiance of the settlers and assured the growth of a strong, homogeneous Union. Thus the Northwest Ordinance tilted the balance of power in North America toward the United States.

The essay by Professor Ruth Bloch examines the evolution of New England missionary activity in the West, 1792–1805. She argues that for several years following the adoption of the Northwest Ordinance eastern religious leaders, especially orthodox Congregational clergymen, were confident that Protestantism would prevail in the West. By the mid-1790s, however, reports of settlers capitulating to "evil" influences and of failure to convert Native Americans alarmed New England clergymen and raised doubts about the future of Christianity in the West. Their uneasiness over these developments was exacerbated by the course of the French Revolution and what it might portend for American society. In response to these challenges, Bloch explains, New England churches created numerous missionary societies, lowered educational standards for ministers, engaged in interdenominational cooperation, looked to the newly established London Missionary Society for guidance, and modified their missionary policy and goals, all of which affected significantly social and religious life on the frontier and on American society generally.

Professor Paul Finkelman's paper focuses on the paradoxical relationship between Article VI of the Northwest Ordinance and the existence of slavery in the western portions of the Old Northwest until 1848. Article VI provided "that there shall be neither slavery nor involuntary servitude" in the Northwest Territory. But that Article, Finkelman cautions, "was not an emancipation proclamation for the Northwest." The reasons for this, he explains, are: (1) the haste of Congress in drafting and approving Article VI without adequate debate; (2) the problem of eradicating an entrenched institution; (3) "serious conflict-of-law questions" inherent in any effort to abolish slavery in an area bounded by slave states; and (4) the unwillingness of many local and national officials to enforce the Ordinance. In developing those points Finkelman stresses pervasive indifference toward exclusion of slavery, the lack of any provision in the Ordinance for an enforcement mechanism, and a poorly drafted document, some provisions of which, notably those pertaining to property rights and the passage on fugitive slaves, undermined the exclusionary statement in Article VI.

Throughout his essay Finkelman demonstrates the weakness of the Ordinance as an antislavery or abolitionist document, and he blasts the myth that it brought a sudden end to slavery in the area north of the Ohio River. At the same time he acknowledges that in the long run the Ordinance "helped put slavery on the road to ultimate extinction" in that area.

The subject of Professor Jurgen Herbst's presentation is higher education in the Old Northwest. He begins by characterizing the Northwest Ordinance and the Morrill Act of 1862 as "the two most important documents in the history of the national government's influence over American higher education." He views Article III of the Ordinance, which provided that "religion, morality, and knowledge, being necessary to good government and the happiness of mankind, schools and the means of education shall forever be encouraged," as a continuation of an historic commitment—a Reformation legacy that was acted upon throughout the colonial period—to the proposition "that secular government and established church were jointly responsible for the establishment, protection, and survival—though not necessarily for the full financial support—of the colleges in their realm." At the same time, he argues, Revolutionary and post-Revolutionary leaders favored a practical education designed to serve the general public over a classical education which prepared a "privileged few . . . for influential positions in government, church, and society." Herbst maintains that despite persistent resistance to change, the Northwest Ordinance and the Morrill Act spurred curricular reforms that demonstrated the ability of popular government to exercise responsible control over higher education.

Herbst traces the varied course of higher education in the Old Northwest from its early phase, during which opposition to tax-supported colleges and universities seriously impeded their growth, through the establishment of state-supported institutions with programs in the liberal arts and sciences, agriculture, engineering, teacher education, and the legal, medical and ministerial professions, and with faculties that engaged in research, curricular development, and in outreach and extension programs. The Hatch Act of 1887 and the

Second Morrill Act of 1890, Herbst concludes, consummated a century-long revolution in higher education during which state-supported colleges and universities became the domain of men and women from all walks of life.

---

1. Phillip R. Shriver, "America's Other Bicentennial," *The Old Northwest: A Journal of Regional Life and Letters*, 9 (Fall 1983): 219–35.

2. The paper presented by Professor David B. Tyack of Stanford Unviersity, "Forming Schools, Forming States: Public Education in a Nation of Republics," could not be published here because of a standing copyright commitment.

I

Ambiguous Achievement: The Northwest Ordinance

JACK N. RAKOVE
Department of History, Stanford University

IN 1971 A DISTINGUISHED GROUP OF HISTORIANS gathered at Williamsburg, Virginia, charged with the task of assessing the remarkable burst of scholarship which had recently produced sweeping reinterpretations of the American Revolution. The honor of presenting the keynote addresses at this conference rightly fell to the two men whose work had precipitated the great transformation of Revolutionary scholarship, Bernard Bailyn and Edmund Morgan. In their papers, both men found occasion to refer to the Northwest Ordinance of 1787, that landmark act of state which is customarily heralded as the one undisputed achievement of the postwar Continental Congress. For Bailyn, the Ordinance's "brilliantly imaginative provisions . . . for opening up new lands in the West and for settling new governments within them" embodied the "expectant stretching and spirited, hopeful striving" which the Revolution had released among Americans of all classes. Morgan, for his part, saw the passage of the Ordinance not only as an affirmation of Revolutionary principles, with the new states and their citizens acquiring an equal status with the original members of the union, but also as an early example of that process of bargaining and compromise that would soon become so essential a feature of American legislative politics.[1]

One doubts whether anyone in the audience raised so much as an eyebrow at these comments. They were entirely consistent with the received view of the Northwest Ordinance, and with the view that prevails today. Three years later, however, a rather different assessment of that act was offered during the course of an exchange between Bailyn and Gary Nash, whose review of the published proceedings of the Williamsburg conference had been less than kind to Bailyn's contribution. In a rejoinder to the letter of protest that Bailyn had submitted to the *William and Mary Quarterly*, Nash raised a new charge. Bailyn's tribute to the opening of the West, he now argued, only revealed the dubious value of a conceptual scheme that "equates 'progress' with the expansion of 'republican' forms of government." Under such a scheme, Nash continued, "Nothing needs to be said about the subjugation of the demographically and technologically weaker peoples who inhabited the Ohio Valley; or about the dictated treaties of 1784–1786; or about the 'brilliantly imaginative' techniques of warfare devised by St. Clair, Wayne, and Clark for the conquest of Indian societies." The movement into the northwest had to be understood for what it was: a renewal of "the lawless white expansion into Indian lands" which Britain had sought to arrest during the decade prior to independence.[2] Far from serving as an example of enlightened legislation, Nash implied, the Northwest Ordinance might better be regarded as a legal facade for the expropriation of Indian lands.

Gary Nash's objections to an uncritical celebration of the Ordinance cannot be dismissed simply as a familiar expression of the radical historiography of the late 1960s and early 1970s. This disparity between the high purposes of the 1787 Ordinance and its ominous implications for native peoples is impossible to ignore. Before the empire of liberty could be extended, extensive

Indian lands had to be liberated, and the history of that struggle is one episode that no bicentennial ought to celebrate. Yet neither will it do to dismiss this famous act of 1787 as simply another step along the trail of tears. For one thing, the aspirations of the Ordinance *were* more noble, more enlightened, than the acquisitive policy it was meant to enforce; for another, had the Ordinance itself never been adopted, had the process of expansion gone forward wholly unchecked—as it inevitably was destined to go forward—the fate of the aboriginal occupants of the Northwest Territory would have been exactly the same.

To strike balances between high aspirations and mundane motives, between great expectations and unintended consequences, is (arguably) what historians like to do best. The inherent ambiguities of the Ordinance emerge if its framing is viewed from three perspectives. One can begin by asking, in the first place, how and why the organization of this territory became so crucial an issue for the American Revolutionaries of the 1770s and 1780s. Second, one can juxtapose the adoption of the Ordinance with the other major event Americans commemorate this year: the Federal Convention of 1787. Finally, a sense of justice requires a return to the issue raised at the outset, in order to examine the less than ambiguous legacy that the Ordinance had for the aboriginal occupants of the Northwest Territory.

At the most general level, the great questions that the Northwest Ordinance ultimately proposed to settle all involved determining exactly how frontier territories would be integrated into a republic founded and controlled by the much longer settled societies along the seaboard. In one sense, the basic issues were political. Would the western territories be admitted to the union on terms of equality with the original thirteen states? Would their residents enjoy the same political rights as their countrymen closer to the Atlantic—or would they suffer something of the same "abridgement of liberties" that Thomas Hutchinson, the last royal governor of

Massachusetts, had mistakenly thought the American colonists should gratefully accept in exchange for the benefits of membership in the British empire?

These were questions that it had become possible even to frame only on the eve of independence. Until fairly late in the colonial period, the question of how the West would be governed had not figured prominently in the politics of either the American colonies or the British empire. In the middle of the eighteenth century, the overwhelming majority of the population still lived huddled close to the Atlantic—in modern terms, a drive of no more than an hour or two from the coast. Where migration had moved inland, the axis of settlement lay along the great river systems—so that access to the coast remained easier than travel into the interior. In their cultural orientation, too, the colonists still faced eastward across the Atlantic, toward the mother country and its great metropolis. The idea that the conquest of the frontier would serve as the great testing point of the American character would have struck many colonists—and especially the articulate, elite classes who dominated public life—as absurd.

The final two decades before Independence, however, brought a sharp and accelerating shift in American interest in the settlement of the interior. The struggle with France for control of the Ohio and upper Mississippi valleys ended in a decisive British victory that lowered the political barriers to movement westward. Perhaps more important, the exponential population growth of the colonies was reinforced by a remarkable upsurge of immigrants from the home islands, and beyond. As Professor Bailyn has noted in his recent study of this migration, a quarter of a million immigrants reached the colonies in the final fifteen years before the outbreak of war in 1775. At least half of these immigrants hailed from protestant Ireland, Scotland, and England; perhaps another third were enslaved Africans; most of the remainder were German protestants. Many of the British and European immigrants headed almost immediately for the frontier: entering through the great ports of Philadelphia and New York, they took up lands in southeastern Pennsylvania, or headed north up the Hudson and then west along the Mohawk; or else they filtered down the Shenandoah Valley and into the southern backcountry as far south as the Carolina and Georgia frontiers, and as far west as Pittsburgh. In their own way, slaves contributed to this migration, too. Their increasing numbers allowed the greater planter families of the tidewater to expand their holdings even further, thus spurring the flight of poorer whites to the frontier—where the planters' younger sons sometimes followed them still, slave gangs in tow.[3] And even in New England, the region that immigrants found entirely unattractive, four generations of fruitful multiplication by the Puritans and their descendants had created a pool of potential emigrants to the West.

The period just before independence, then, saw a major leap in the area of eastern America opened for settlement. It inspired ambitious and complex speculative schemes, as entrepreneurs well aware of rising land values in the east foresaw the profits to be made from the settlement of the West. Perhaps most important, it was this surge of settlement that first raised some of the key political problems that the framers of the Ordinance of 1787 would have to grapple with more than a decade later. Three of these sets of problems deserve particular mention.

The first set of problems stemmed from the simple difficulty that existing authorities experienced in keeping up with the rapid pace of migration and in providing a working framework of basic institutions for the frontier. To organize even the minimal apparatus of government was a daunting task, especially because, outside New England, the sheer physical dispersal of settlement made it difficult for legally constituted authorities to maintain ready access to the population. Churches—which might have been expected to step into the vacuum left by government—faced even greater problems.

Dispersed populations could barely assemble for services; frontier settlers were ill prepared to defray the costs of hiring a minister; and even if they were, a severe shortage of ordained ministers made it difficult to find one.[4]

Even after a rudimentary set of local institutions could be organized, it remained to be decided—in the second place—how frontier settlements were to be incorporated into the larger provincial communities of which they were nominally a part. Would interior areas be granted equal rights of representation in the colonial (or later the state) assemblies? Royal governors were under instructions to limit the size of the colonial legislatures in order to make those truculent bodies more manageable; frontier settlements were sometimes the victims of this limitation. But the political questions also touched the conduct of local affairs. Would these settlements gain effective control over local institutions of government, or would these be staffed by men who owed their loyalty not to local interests but to the existing colonial authorities further east? Would there, in other words, be two classes of citizenship within any colony or state: a superior status reserved for residents living in the original settlements, an inferior one relegated to migrants along the frontier?[5]

This question in turn implicated a third set of issues. It was one thing to extend equal political rights and the effective support of church and state to one's own descendants moving west. But to the extent that settlement along the frontier depended disproportionately on new and strange groups, it was not immediately apparent why they deserved the same rights and privileges of the predominantly English groups whose forebears had come first. It was no less enlightened a spokesman for the rising glory of America than Benjamin Franklin who as early as 1751 wondered (in his essay *Observations Concerning the Increase of Mankind*) why Pennsylvania should even welcome the "Palatine Boors" and other "swarthy" peoples who were swarming into the colony.

Good and sober workers they might well be; but how could these people, with their strange customs and language, ever be integrated into the existing society? And conversely, what loyalty did these new groups in turn owe to the established authorities in any particular colony or state? There was never any love to be lost between the Anglophobic Scots-Irish Presbyterians who were scattered from Pennsylvania south, on the one hand, and the creolized English Americans who dominated the colonies in which they settled.

This concern with the assimilation of alien population elements was genuine and plausible, and it was recognized as such by other observers, who, however, sometimes looked ahead more optimistically than Franklin was originally disposed to do. In his famous *Letters from an American Farmer,* Hector St. John de Crevecoeur had rightly asked what allegiance the displaced peasants of Europe owed to the countries from which they had fled to come to America.

> What attachment can a poor European emigrant have for a country in which he had nothing? The knowledge of the language, the love of a few kindred as poor as himself, were the only cords that tied him; his country is now that which gives him his land, bread, protection, and consequence; *Ubi panis ibi patria* is the motto of all emigrants.

But allegiance to particular governments, Crevecoeur also understood, would not come into existence immediately. "Europeans submit insensibly" to the new conditions under which they found themselves living in America, he observed; and then, "in the course of a few generations," they would become "not only Americans in general, but either Pennsylvanians, Virginians, or provincials under some other name."[6] Their first loyalties would be to the New World itself, Crevecoeur implied; more immediate and particularistic allegiances would follow only in time.

Compounding all of these problems was the one additional factor that would most powerfully affect the creation of the national domain after independence. The rights of government that individual colonies and states claimed over the interior rested on the swampy soil of seventeenth-century charters and other tenuous claims. These were weak reeds on which to lean when dealing with migrants who owed little if any inherent loyalty to the existing political elites. If the existing provinces could extend their jurisdiction into the interior, then the allegiances of the frontiersman might be secured; but the question remained, could those jurisdictions be established?[7]

All of these issues were somehow involved in the post-revolutionary efforts to organize the frontier, but the one that mattered most was the question of jurisdiction. As is well known, the basic struggle over the future of the West lay between two blocs of states: the landed states of Virginia, North Carolina, Massachusetts, Connecticut, Georgia, and New York, who had claims of greater and lesser merit to extensive lands in the interior; and the landless states of Pennsylvania, Delaware, Rhode Island, New Jersey, and Maryland, whose western boundaries were clearly set by their colonial charters. In practical terms, the dispute centered on the question of when, and under what conditions, the landed states would cede their claims to the union, thereby creating a national domain that could in turn be organized into new states.

None of the landed states' claims seemed particularly persuasive, if taken on their merits. Notions of North American geography had not attained the level even of crude knowledge when sea-to-sea clauses were placed in the original charters of Virginia, Massachusetts, and Connecticut. Yet when independence was declared, Virginia insisted that its claim to the territory northwest of the Ohio River had to be honored. Meanwhile, Massachusetts and Connecticut were preparing to jump over New York in order to reactivate claims that would begin somewhere around the Finger Lakes and run west through lakes Erie, Huron and Michigan until they hit the western boundary of the new republic—wherever that might turn out to be. And New York was in a class by itself. Lacking a formal charter, it rested its claims first on its special political relationship with the Six Nations of the Iroquois confederacy and then on the Iroquois claim to supremacy over the western tribes above the Ohio.

This conflict between landed and landless states was the dominant practical problem that the framers of the Articles of Confederation had to face. In an effort to provide a painless solution to the enormous financial burdens the war promised to create, the landless states sought from the outset to give the Continental Congress broad power to limit state boundaries and to control the national domain that would be created beyond. They rested their case on three main points. They argued, first, that the purported boundaries set by the colonial charters were both fanciful and unreasonable; second, that the actual control of this territory could be wrenched from Great Britain only through the united force of all the states, who should therefore acquire joint title to the entire region; and third, that the recognition of these individual state claims would work a basic injustice. The landed states could defray much of their share of the costs of war simply by selling territory; the landless states, by contrast, would have to levy heavy taxes— and thus perhaps force their own citizens to emigrate to the lands of their better circumstanced neighbors.

Against these claims, which seem so equitable on their face, the landed states literally held their ground. They succeeded in pruning almost every clause relating to western lands from the final draft of the Articles of Confederation that Congress submitted to the states in November 1777. In doing so, they did not deny that a national domain should eventually be created; they implied only that its existence would depend on the voluntary cessions of the claiming states.

It is an open question how this process would have unfolded had the Revolutionary War been brought to a

speedy and victorious conclusion in, say, 1778. Then,
perhaps, the landed states might have pursued a narrow
but rigid notion of self-interest and clung to their
claims. But as the war dragged indecisively on, two
factors worked to give the idea of a national domain a
deeper and more urgent appeal. One was the refusal of
the Maryland legislature to ratify the Articles of Confederation until the landed states—especially Virginia—had indicated they were prepared to cede their
claims to the lands beyond the Ohio to the union. In
fact, it was only in 1781 that Maryland finally relented
and the Articles took effect.[8]

But the second and more important sets of factors
were those at work among the leaders of the landed
states themselves. By the fall of 1779, the continental
dollar was virtually worthless, and the threat of bank-
ruptcy concentrated congressional thinking wonder-
fully. Henceforth it proved impossible for any member
of Congress, whatever his state, to avoid seeing the
creation of a national domain as a great financial pan-
acea. Calls for state cessions were now being heard,
Philip Schuyler informed the New York assembly, not
only from delegates from the landless states, but also
from "Gentlemen who represented States in Circumstances seemingly similar to our's."[9] The assembly responded promptly by approving an act of cession in early
1780; and within months, Virginia followed suit.

Now, there is obviously a great deal more that can be
said about the politics of creating the national domain.
Sordid considerations of interest played their role, but so
did deeply principled convictions about the difficulty
that republics faced in governing extensive territories.
But the most important point to be stressed involves
understanding the way in which the process of creating
a national domain forced political leaders to fashion a
new and more sophisticated notion of the national interest than had prevailed at the outset of the Revolution.

When the dispute over the control of the western
lands had first erupted in Congress in 1776, it had posed

the single greatest obstacle not only to the completion of the Articles of Confederation, but arguably to the survival of the nation. But by the time Virginia tendered its final cession to Congress in the fall of 1783, the need to develop the West arguably provided the strongest set of shared concerns that would bind the union together now that the great issue of independence had at last been resolved. True, suspicions and resentments continued to linger. Key New York leaders, for example, remained embittered over Congress's failure to support their well-established claim to Vermont; and until Virginia relinquished the hold it had retained over Kentucky, many small state leaders remained fearful that this one state would exert inordinate influence over the postwar development of the country.

But on balance, the hard bargaining and endless maneuvering that preceded the formal creation of the Northwest Territory in 1784 had to be viewed in another light. If this seemingly intractable issue could finally be resolved in favor of the confederation, might it not prove a model for common sense and compromise in other disputed areas as well? Throughout this struggle, key leaders on both sides of the question had been forced to weigh national and state interests quite carefully. At times they had acted as the literal attorneys for their states, insisting, as the Virginia delegates continually had to do, that cessions could be completed only if the conditions Virginia imposed were accepted. But on other occasions they had been required to speak to their constituents on behalf of some larger notion of the national interest—to act, in other words, not merely as the ambassadors from semi-sovereign states, but also as virtuous legislators who had to explain to their constituents where the greater interest of the national community lay.

It was, in short, the essentially political character of this process that made the creation of the national domain so notable an achievement. Ordinarily when we think of the virtues of the Northwest Ordinance, the capstone of that achievement, we call attention to the various liberal principles it espouses in its call for education and for humane dealings with the Indians, its enumeration of basic civil liberties (including rights of conscience), its repudiation of slavery, and its promise of early statehood. But in a more basic sense, the deeper achievement of the Ordinance lay in the ease of its final passage. By the time the Ordinance was formally enacted on Friday the 13th of July 1787, it could best be described (as Jack Eblen has noted) as "a rather ordinary piece of noncontroversial legislation."[10]

Given the enormous difficulties that Congress had met in literally all of its other efforts to frame and implement broad national policy, this was nothing short of remarkable. In 1781 and again in 1783, Congress had asked the states to vest it with independent authority to levy an impost duty, but those requests had never secured the unanimous ratification that the Articles of Confederation required. In 1784 it had proposed additional amendments in the area of foreign commerce; those, too, had foundered. Its efforts to persuade North Carolina and Georgia to refrain from confiscating Indian lands had been rebuffed, with the result that war threatened along the southern frontier. And in 1786 the bitter debate that Secretary of Foreign Affairs John Jay had launched by urging the southern states to renounce the navigation of the Mississippi River in order to facilitate the completion of a commercial treaty with Spain had produced a stark sectional division within Congress, with the five states from Maryland south arrayed against the eight states from Delaware north.

Against this pathetic background, then, the plans for the Northwest Territory seemed a beacon of hope. But the fulfillment of that hope was in turn dependent on finding a solution to all those other problems that had reduced Congress to a condition—as contemporaries put it—of "imbecility." The mere enactment of provisions for territorial government and settlement could not guarantee that Congress would actually be able to discharge its mandate effectively. Would the flood of migrants already streaming west maintain their loyalty to a union incapable either of defending the frontiers against the increasingly hostile tribes on both sides of the Ohio, or of forcing Spain to reopen the Mississippi to American navigation? Would the lands of the North-west Territory be preserved for orderly settlement if the handful of American troops policing the Ohio failed to prevent settlers from squatting on lands or provoking increased Indian resistance? To prime the pump of west-ern lands, which many still regarded as the financial salvation of the union, Congress needed revenue to maintain an adequate military establishment in the Ohio Valley. But that was what it most lacked and had no immediate prospect of attaining—unless, of course, the great Convention meeting at Philadelphia suc-ceeded in framing a constitution that would reinvigo-rate the entire federal system.

Without the Constitution, then, the Northwest Or-dinance would have been little more than a dead letter. If Congress could not deliver upon its promise to defend the West and regulate its settlement, it would find itself no more immune to the fickle loyalties of migrants—the least loyal of men—than individual states had been over the previous decades. Only by endowing the na-tional government with the means to act on its inten-tions could the Federal Convention redeem the promise that the Northwest Ordinance held out. Should the Convention fail in its task, it was thus entirely conceiv-able that Britain and Spain would emerge as the domi-nant political forces in the interior of the continent, leaving the original states clinging to the ocean, de-prived of the resources of the West, and at loggerheads over all the other issues that had divided them since war's end.

The Convention solved these problems, of course, by granting the new national government the full authority it required to collect its own revenues and make and enforce its own laws. But no less important was its conscious decision to treat the future states of the West in the same liberal way that the Ordinance envisioned. The issue was posed directly during the critical first fortnight in July, when the delegates tried to determine how representation in the lower house of Congress would be apportioned.

What is noteworthy about this debate is the candor with which the delegates considered whether or not the new states of the West should be treated equally with the existing members of the union. Gouverneur Morris repeatedly put the point directly. In his view,

> the rule of representation ought to be so fixed as to secure to the Atlantic states a prevalence in the National Councils. The new States will know less of the public interest than these, will have an interest in many respects different, in particular will be little scrupulous of involving the Community in wars the burdens & operations of which would fall chiefly on the maritime States.

Morris proposed two alternative means for securing the interests of the Atlantic states. Either the Constitution could allocate seats in a way that would explicitly protect the numerical security of the seaboard states; or else it should leave it to future legislatures to determine whether reapportionment was necessary. This, of course, would allow the original majority to perpetuate its rule regardless of the movement of population.

Such candor elicited equally blunt responses. Morris claimed, for example, that the interior settlements "would not be able to furnish men equally enlightened, to share in the administration of our common interests" because, after all, "The busy haunts of men not the remote wilderness, was the proper school of political talents." Madison immediately asked Morris whether he "determined the human character by the points of the compass," and then went on to insist "that no unfavorable distinctions were admissible either in point of justice or policy." And Madison's colleague, the crusty George Mason, put the issue even more directly. "Ought we to sacrifice what we know to be right," Mason asked, "lest it should prove favorable to states which are not yet in existence?" If the Convention did otherwise, he warned, the frontier settlements "will either not unite or will speedily revolt from the Union, if they are not in all respects placed on an equal footing."[11]

Mason and Madison spoke on July 11, two days before Congress would adopt the Ordinance ninety miles away in New York. It does not go too far to suggest that the two Virginians grasped the central issue with almost perfect understanding. Equal rights of government and representation were demanded, as Madison noted, by "justice and policy" alike. He could as easily have said that policy demanded justice. The allegiance of the West could never be secured simply by giving the union the authority and resources it required to police the frontier. Loyalty required equality: the granting of equal political rights would, Madison believed, bind the mobile men of the frontier to the older communities they had left behind.

This conviction that interior states could not be organized as inferior states was the central principle that the Ordinance endorsed as a matter of policy and the Constitution reinforced as a matter of principle. But, also, its liberal thrust is belied by one further presumption that guided all western policy throughout the Revolutionary era and well beyond.

Americans described the lands lying beyond the line of settlements as "wastelands" or as "unappropriated" lands. But of course they were occupied by Indian nations who rightfully regarded their ancestral homelands as their own. Federal policy toward these native occupants was clouded by two factors. First, the relevant clause of the Articles of Confederation did not provide Congress with clear or undisputed authority to control Indian relations. Its broad grant of a "sole and exclusive right and power of . . . regulating the trade and managing all affairs with the Indians" was sharply compromised by two additional qualifications limiting congressional jurisdiction to Indians "not members of any of the states" and "further "provid[ing] that the legislative right of any State within its own limits be not infringed or violated." In practical terms, Congress could exercise effective jurisdiction over Indian affairs only within the national domain—only, in other words, after the states had voluntarily surrendered their claims.

Yet even after the creation of the national domain gave Congress the "sole right and power" to manage Indian affairs in the Northwest Territory, its efforts to exercise its authority was marred by a second defect. With its own treasury empty, Congress balked at the idea of purchasing the tribal lands it coveted. Instead, it preferred to insist, first, that title to these lands had been transferred to the United States by Great Britain in the peace treaty; and second, that the defeated hostile tribes—the four Iroquois tribes who had sided with the British and their western allies—had to relinquish their claims because they were a conquered people. At the treaties of Fort Stanwix and Fort McIntosh, the federal commissioners dealt in a harsh and preemptory fashion with the Indians, literally commanding them to cede the vast tracts Congress desired. Too stunned by this policy and the news of their abandonment by Great Britain to resist, the cowed Indian nations initially acceded to these demands, but by the time the Ordinance was passed in July 1787, a militant reaction was setting in among the tribes of the Ohio Valley. Open hostilities were still two years away, but the dangers inherent in the federal theory of cession by conquest were rapidly becoming evident.[12]

It is against this perspective that the famous third article of the Northwest Ordinance must be seen.

> The utmost good faith shall always be observed towards the Indians; their lands and property shall never be taken from them without their consent; and in their property, rights and liberty they never shall be invaded or disturbed, unless in just and lawful wars authorized by Congress; but laws founded in justice and humanity shall, from time to time, be made, for preventing wrongs being done to them, and for preserving peace and friendship with them.

One can indeed see this declaration as a mark of the reassessment of the naive and unjust assumptions upon which Congress had first acted toward the defeated tribes at war's end. The notion that "good faith" and voluntary "consent" should be the basic elements of all dealings with the Indians—as self-evident as that truth might seem today—was something that the Revolutionaries still had to establish in theory and then confirm in practice. Unfortunately, the first of these steps proved easier than the second.

All laws are statements of policy, but policies do not always abide by law. Again, the hopeful intentions of the Ordinance were mocked by the practical factors that operated along the frontier. Colonel Josiah Harmar and his modest contingent of continental troops could not police the entire frontier or prevent eager settlers from rushing into the territory and exacerbating the already mounting fears of the native tribes. Nor could Congress bring itself to undo the damage its initial policy had worked. Nothing in the Northwest Ordinance prevented the further deterioration of relations that led to the brutal and violent frontier war of the early 1790s.

Nor, at a more fundamental level, did the "enlightenment" of Article III succeed in shaking the deeper assumption upon which policy toward the Indians had rested since 1783. At war's end, Congress had solicited the advice of two of its leading Indian experts—George Washington and Philip Schuyler. Washington had originally contemplated a fairly aggressive policy toward the defeated tribes, resting in part on the establishment of military colonies along the frontier that would serve to deter Indian violence and drive the tribes away from the line of settlement. Schuyler, in a more influential letter, offered a more calculated response. A militant policy would be expensive and dangerous, he argued; it would also be unnecessary. Instead, he recommended a gradual expansion of the line of settlement, conducted in a way that would not alarm the Indians overmuch and that would allow for the orderly extension of federal authority. The great advantage of this policy, Schuyler concluded, was that it would lead to the peaceful retreat of the Indians. As the line of settlement advanced, their supplies of game would be exhausted, and the Indians would simply move further westward, leaving other tracts of land to be acquired at the trifling expense of a purchase. And one day, the Indians would simply be gone—north to Canada, or west of the Mississippi.[13]

This was the deeper purpose that even the enlightened Northwest Ordinance was designed to serve. Its provisions solved the problem of the frontier by offering a means both to extend the empire of liberty and to incorporate these liberated territories into the extended republic that Madison and his colleagues at Philadelphia were busy creating. But here as elsewhere, one people's liberty was another people's loss. That may have been the most obvious meaning of the Northwest Ordinance; it was arguably its most important, and probably its most tragic.

---

1. Bernard Bailyn, "The Central Themes of the American Revolution: An Interpretation," and Edmund S. Morgan, "Conflict and Consensus in the American Revolution," are both printed in Stephen G. Kurtz and James H. Hutson, eds., *Essays on the American Revolution* (Chapel Hill, 1973), for the passages cited, see 20, 306–7.

2. The original Nash review is in *William and Mary Quarterly*, 3d ser., 31 (1974): 311–14; the exchange between Bailyn and Nash is ibid. 32 (1975): 182–85.

3. Bernard Bailyn, *Voyagers to the West: A Passage in the Peopling of America on the Eve of the Revolution* (New York, 1986), 24–28.

4. The classic illustration of these problems can be found in the Anglican missionary Charles Woodmason's account of his activities in the Carolina backcountry. See Richard Hooker, ed., *Carolina Backcountry on the Eve of the Revolution; The Journal and Other Writings of Charles Woodmason, Anglican Itinerant* (Chapel Hill, 1953).

5. The differences between the two Regulation movements in North and South Carolina illustrate these complementary aspects of the problem of organizing the frontier; see, in general, Richard M. Brown, *The South Carolina Regulators* (Cambridge, 1963); and A. Roger Ekirch, Jr., *"Poor Carolina": Politics and Society in Colonial North Carolina, 1729–1776* (Chapel Hill, 1981).

6. J. Hector St. John De Crevecoeur, *Letters from an American Farmer...*, ed. Albert E. Stone (New York, 1981), 69, 73.

7. Here as in later sections I rely on the analysis in Peter S. Onuf, *The Origins of the Federal Republic: Jurisdictional Controversies in the United States, 1775–1787* (Philadelphia, 1983).

8. On the framing of the Articles of Confederation, see Jack N. Rakove, *The Beginnings of National Politics: An Interpretive History of the Continental Congress* (New York, 1979), chaps. 7–8. The politics of western lands is extensively treated in Thomas Perkins Abernethy, *Western Lands and the American Revolution* (New York, 1937); and see Merrill Jensen, *The Articles of Confederation: An Interpretation of the Social-Constitutional History of the American Republic, 1774–1781* (Madison, 1940), and "The Creation of the National Domain, 1781–1784," *Mississippi Valley Historical Review,* 26 (December 1939): 323–42.

9. Philip Schuyler to the Lieutenant Governor and the Speaker of the Assembly of New York, 29 January 1780, in Edmund C. Burnett, ed., *Letters of Members of the Continental Congress* (Washington, D.C., 1921-1936), 5:29–31.

10. Jack Eblen, *The First and Second United States Empires: Governors and Territorial Government, 1784–1912* (Pittsburgh, 1968), 17–51; and see Robert F. Berkhofer, Jr., "Jefferson, the Ordinance of 1784, and the Origins of the American Territorial System," *William and Mary Quarterly,* 3d ser., 29 (April 1972): 231–62; and Arthur Bestor, "Constitutionalism and the Settlement of the West: The Attainment of Consensus, 1754–1784," in John Porter Bloom, ed., *The American Territorial System* (Athens, Ohio, 1973), 13–44.

11. Max Farrand, ed., *The Records of the Federal Convention of 1787,* 2d rev. ed. (New Haven, 1987), 1:533–34, 578, 583–85.

12. The best short account of these developments is in Reginald Horsman, *Expansion and American Indian Policy* (East Lansing, 1969).

13. For the key expressions of these ideas, see Philip Schuyler to the President of Congress, 29 July 1783, Papers of the Continental Congress, item 153, vol. 3, f. 601–8, National Archives; George Washington to James Duane, 7 September 1783, in John C. Fitzpatrick, ed., *The Writings of George Washington* (Washington, D.C., 1931–44), 27:133–40; and Henry Knox, Report to the President, 15 June 1789, in *American State Papers: Indian Affairs,* 1:13–15.

II

The Northwest Ordinance and the Balance of Power in North America

GORDON T. STEWART
Department of History, Michigan State University

"TO BEGIN WITH, HISTORY IS ALL GEOGRAPHY."
So thought the great nineteenth-century historian Jules
Michelet and, when evaluating the significance of the
Northwest Ordinance, it is essential to begin with geography. In recent times, the area bounded by the Ohio,
the upper Mississippi and the Great Lakes is not a part of
the world normally viewed as strategically significant.
In contrast to geo-political hot spots like the Middle
East, the Old Northwest is quiet and innocuous. But
one of the fundamental reasons for the Middle East
turmoil, as the British military historian John Keegan
has pointed out, is that the region is at the crossroads of
continents. Asia and Europe and Africa meet in the
Middle East and the history of the region is characterized by the ebb and flow of empires as rival powers
and religions have struggled to control this critical piece
of geography. When the Northwest Ordinance was passed in 1787, the region it applied to was similar to the
modern Middle East. The area between the Ohio and
the Lakes was at the crossroads of empires. The French
and the British had clashed and competed in the Ohio

and Lakes country in the 1740s and 1750s; the new British empire in Canada worked to keep out American settlement from the 1760s to the 1790s; the Spanish in Louisiana crept up the Mississippi and held out attractive inducements to the trans-Appalachian settlers to throw in their lot with the southern river route out of the West.

Because of the subsequent disposition of the region, incorporated into the expanding United States empire, the significance of the Old Northwest in terms of continental geography is under appreciated. Before the advent of canals and railroads from the 1820s onwards, the quickest, cheapest and most natural routes into and out of the Northwest were by the Mississippi and the St. Lawrence, the two great water highways into the interior of the continent. Fort Mackinac is viewed by modern eyes as sitting remotely at the northern tip of the Michigan peninsula, but if a direct line east is taken by the Ottawa River it lands in Montreal. Such key points in the Northwest as Mackinac influenced an immense region in the late eighteenth and early nineteenth centuries—from Montreal across to the next major mountain range, the Rockies. As late as 1815, James Monroe could still remind John Quincy Adams that "the connection with and commanding influence of Mackinac with the several tribes of Indians inhabiting the country within our limits between the Lakes and the Rocky Mountains has been long felt and known."[1] In 1787, the American hold on this strategic region was not secure. In addition to the resistance presented by the indigenous Indian peoples, the British colony at Quebec extended like a dagger into the territory of the Old Northwest. The modern peninsula of Ontario (created as a separate colony of Upper Canada by the British) lay directly east of much of the technically American territory. It was settled by anti-American loyalists and garrisoned by British regulars in systematic contact with the Indian peoples throughout American territory. In short, the Old Northwest was an insecure appendage of the new United States subjected to foreign influences, foreign attack and internal violence.

This insecurity affecting the Old Northwest was even more threatening because the United States itself was still struggling to become a viable state. It is difficult for us to appreciate the full significance of the weak condition of the new nation in the 1780s because the United States became so quickly the dominant power in North America. But that future powerful status was by no means a self-evident outcome for those living in the difficult post-war years. The new nation faced rampant inflation of the paper money issued by the Continental Congress, huge debts were owed to France and Holland, the rebellion led by Daniel Shays in western Massachusetts confirmed the existence of serious internal problems. The forecast by British critics that the United States would soon collapse seemed to be bearing out. As George Washington lamented, he was "mortified beyond expression that in the moment of our acknowledged independence we should by our conduct verify the predictions of our transatlantic foe and render ourselves ridiculous and contemptible in the eyes of all Europe."[2] It was in this troubled context that the members of Congress discussed the need for a policy on the western territories. In a letter of 28 September 1786, the Rhode Island delegates reported back to Governor John Collins of Rhode Island the issues facing the Congress. They explained that "an ordinance for the establishing of a colonial Government in the western territoryes is now nearly compleated." They proceeded to refer yet again to the exhausted federal treasury and the loss of credit with foreign powers and they added a gloomy postscript that "an enemy on our frontiers stands prepared to take every advantage of our prostrate condition."[3]

There was a further factor in the circumstances of the western territories that intensified the uncertainty about its future. This was the allegiance of the settlers moving into the region. In this period, national allegiance was still forming. Many of the new settlers, groups like the Scotch Irish, for example, had no strong commitment to the new United States. And there are other examples from the period that show how easily loyalties could shift or could be influenced by land ownership issues. In the British colony of Nova Scotia, twelve thousand pre-1776 New England settlers became loyal British subjects in spite of extensive links with the new states. In Upper Canada, about four-fifths of the population on the eve of the war of 1812 were American settlers who had come in after the initial loyalist migration. The British Commander-in-Chief in Upper Canada, General Isaac Brock, questioned the loyalty of these settlers but they did not go over to the invading Americans because their titles to the rich bottom lands of western Upper Canada depended on British control of the area. In a sweeping arc of country from Nova Scotia to Upper Canada to the Old Northwest, around the periphery of the new United States, the allegiance of the mobile settler communities was uncertain.[4] Their connection with eastern government was tenuous; everything depended on what authority could be established in the area to guarantee and protect their land. Some sense of the uncertainty about allegiance can be gained from James Madison's ruminating on the spread of unrest in the eastern states. Writing to Edward Pendleton in February 1787, Madison, in a pessimistic frame of mind, worried that "the late turbulent scenes in Massachusetts and the infamous ones in Rhode Island have done inexpressible injury to the republican character of that part of the United States and a propensity towards monarchy is said to have been produced in some leading minds."[5] If even in the heartland of republican America there was a possibility of allegiance to monarchy returning, how much more so was it a possibility that the allegiance of remote, dissatisfied western settlers might turn in non-American directions?

These, then, are three cardinal points to bear in mind when assessing the context within which the

Northwest Ordinance was debated—the Old Northwest was a critical area strategically; the United States
was engaged in a difficult struggle for survival; and the
allegiance of expanding settler communities caught between American and British spheres of influence was
uncertain and still forming.

In such circumstances American leaders were realis-
tic in their assessment of the new nation's place in North
America. Given the weaknesses in the new nation, they
understood the need to counter any British or Spanish
attempts to tilt the balance of power toward their impe-
rial holdings. To modern minds, it seems distinctly odd
to think in terms of a balance of power in North America, but to policy-makers in the late eighteenth and
early nineteenth centuries, such concepts were a natural part of the world in which they lived. Kenneth
Bourne, in his *Great Britain and the Balance of Power in
North America,* has shown that down to the Civil War
period, Britain garrisoned Canada, prepared war plans
and built canals as elements in a general policy of
keeping a counterweight to the United States.[6] British
interest in Texas in the 1830s should also be viewed in
this light. Thomas Jefferson was keenly aware of these
considerations and quite open in expressing his views on
the need of the United States to understand how power
was deployed on the continent. As Secretary of State in
Washington's first administration, he made plain to
Gouverneur Morris his fear of British power building up
by incorporating Spanish territory from the Mississippi
to Nootka Sound. Jefferson warned Morris that "the
consequences of their [the British] acquiring all the
territory on our frontier from the St. Croix to the St.
Marys are too obvious to you to need development; you
would readily see the dangers that would then environ
us." Jefferson summed up by making the point that "a
due balance on our borders is not less desirable to us
than a balance of power in Europe has always appeared
to them."[7]

This sense of insecurity was intensified, of course,

because of actual British policy from Canada. The British still retained possession of the northwest posts; she continued to build relationships with the Indian peoples in the Northwest. The strengthening of the garrisons and the forward policy of Lieutenant-Governor James Simcoe (especially after 1791) bespoke a determination to keep up the military pressure on the western fringes of the United States. The presence of anti-American loyalists was seen as a further pressure on Britain to act aggressively in the West. As John Jay reviewed British policy in September 1785, he sketched out the pattern that was developing. "The Detention of the Posts, the strengthening of the garrisons in our Neighbourhood and various other circumstances bespeak a language very different from that of kindness and good will." In seeking explanations for such behavior, Jay turned to the loyalists. "I am well informed," he told John Adams, "that some of the Loyalists advise and warmly press for the Detention of the Posts. It is strange that Men who for ten Years have done Nothing but deceive should still retain any Credit."[8] From his watching point in London in 1785, Adams confirmed reports "of a general Confederation of the Indian Nations against the United States, which the Refugees propagate, partly for the Pleasure they take in the thought and partly to persuade the Government to build Ships and forts upon the Lakes, Services in which they hope to get employment under the Crown and the Fingering of some of its Money." They think, added Adams, that "they may play with us as they please" because the new States were not united enough to respond.[9]

John Jay kept this view of British policy before the members of Congress. In a report presented in March 1786, he outlined British military preparations in Canada and the state of military readiness of the forts. "The number of forces stationed in the Province of Quebec" suggested what British intentions were. "The Asperity observable in the British Nation towards us," continued Jay, "creates Suspicions that they wish to see our Difficulties of every kind increase and multiply."[10] By beefing up its military presence and championing the cause of the Indians, the British were trying to disengage much of the Northwest from American authority. When William Pitt, the British Prime Minister, proposed to mediate between Americans and Indians, Gouverneur Morris knew what they were up to. "If all this be true," he explained to President Washington, "[Pitt's] game is evident. The Mediation is to be with us a Price for adopting his Plans and with the Indian Tribes a Means of constituting himself their Patron and Protector. It may be proper to combine all this with the late Division of Canada and the present measures for the Military organisation of the Upper Country."[11]

As evidence piled up, American leaders became convinced that there had been a systematic policy since 1783 by the British and the loyalist lackies to detach the western parts of the United States. In a succinct but cogent report to the French Committee of Public Safety in 1795, James Monroe, then U.S. Minister to France, set out the case:

> With this view [of separating the west] she refused to surrender the forts, excited the Indians to make war on our families, encouraged Spain to refuse our right to the Navigation of the Mississippi. [Great Britain will use the unease of the western people over the navigation issue] and improve it into an opportunity of separating the new from the old states and connecting them with her interests in Canada. . . . Next to conquest, separation would be the most advantageous for Britain [who would] become the ally of the western states and play them off against the eastern.[12]

This fear of dismemberment in the West was confirmed by the course of Vermont which seemed to be gravitating in 1787 toward the British in Canada. "The English," Jay warned Jefferson in April 1787, "are making some important settlements on the River St. Lawrence—many of our people go there and it is said that Vermont is not greatly inclined to be the fourteenth state. Taxes and relaxed governments agree but ill."[13] In another letter to Jefferson on this theme, Jay argued that Britain was promulgating the idea that "the Interests of the Atlantic and Western Parts of the United States are distinct and that the growth of the latter will tend to diminish that of the former. . . . If Britain really means us harm she will adopt and impress this Idea."[14]

The issue of western separation was linked to alleged British intervention in the troubles in the eastern states, especially Shays' rebellion. In December 1786, Jay was convinced that "a variety of considerations afford room for Suspicion that there is an Understanding between the Insurgents in Massachusetts and some leading persons in Canada."[15] Edward Carrington, part of the Virginia delegation to Congress, told Edmund Randolph, the Governor of Virginia, that "it is said a British influence is operating in this mischievous affair. . . . It is an undoubted truth that communications are held by Lord Dorchester with both the Vermonters and the insurgents of Massachusetts and that a direct offer has been made to the latter of the protection and Government of Great Britain." Once again, Carrington perceived a grand British plan in all this. "That Great Britain," he insisted in December 1786, "will be in readiness to improve any advantage which our derangements may present for regaining her lost dominions, we are not to doubt. All her appointments to her Colonies, as well as Missions into these States, are calculated to this object."[16] Henry Lee added his weight to that view that there was "authentic information that the malcontents contemplate a re-union with Great Britain."[17]

Far across the Appalachians, the British influence was also seen to be at work in Kentucky and the Ohio Valley. Edward Rutledge complained in 1794 that "British influence has been tampering with the people of Kentucky and of the neighborhood of Pittsburg, to seduce them from the United States or to encourage them in a revolt against the general government."[18] The *New York Daily Advertiser*, on 23 February 1789, printed an item expressing similar fears about western separation. "By information received from Kentucky," began the article, "we learn that many of the principal people of that district are warmly in favor of a separation from the Union and contend that it is injurious to the interests of that country to be connected with the Atlantic states. This idea [is] so pregnant with mischief to America."[19]

These fears of a British master plan to encircle the new nation, stir up internal rebellions and dismember the western territories from the eastern states were exaggerated but they were not without foundation. British officials in Canada like James Simcoe did in fact pursue aggressive interventionist policies and, as late as 1814 during the peace negotiations at Ghent, the British proposed the creation of a large Indian buffer state in the Northwest as a permanent barrier to future American expansion in that direction. John Quincy Adams believed British policy to be based on "a longing to stunt their [the United States'] growth."[20] As J. C. A. Stagg has shown in his recent work on the War of 1812, the American government had a specific fear of British plans to build up her power in Canada from which base they would be able to influence the great western territories of the United States.[21] That shrewd observer of nations, Albert Gallatin, believed in 1814 that "it is now evident that Great Britain intends to aggrandize herself in North America."[22] In short, throughout the entire 1783–1815 period, American policymakers and influential members of Congress convinced themselves that the British were using their position in Canada to break the western territories away from the fragile union of eastern states.

The Northwest Ordinance takes on special significance when placed in this setting. The Congress of the United States might have decided that the new nation's eastern problems were so pressing that all attempts to control and administer the western territories should be abandoned or at least postponed. Congress might have decided that the region was so vulnerable to Indian and British threats that it should simply become a military preserve until Americans had gained the upper hand.

But Congress took neither of these options. They decided for an effective land settlement scheme that would reassure existing settlers, attract new settlers and help reduce the national debt. In doing so, Congress arrived at a solution that swung the Old Northwest's allegiance decisively to the United States.

Once the western territories had been ceded to the United States, they might have been treated simply as conquered territory within which settlers had no rights and which might well be governed on a military-colonial basis. This concept that the Old Northwest was conquered territory (notwithstanding the old charter claims to the west) was made explicit by William Grayson during a debate in May 1786. "The Quebeck Act [1774] took in all that Country," he reminded delegates, "and Virginia had a right to what she conquered with her own arms and the United States had a right to all the rest of the territory by Conquest."[23] The way in which Britain had treated Canada following the conquest of 1760 was a contemporary precedent for the victorious power setting up a new government on its own terms. And in the 1760s, the New England settlers who moved to Nova Scotia considered all their traditional rights (such as township government) had been lost because they were moving to territory conquered by the British and therefore disposable of by Britain as she thought fit. Members of Congress were familiar, of course, with colonial control and, in their discussions of the disposition of the western territory, they used the phrase "the establishing of a colonial Government in the western territory" or "a Collonial Government for the western country."[24] In this eighteenth-century context then, the western lands could have been held for a long period under the dependent, colonial tutelage of the United States.

This possibility of keeping the western territories in an inactive, dependent relationship with the eastern states was given support by those who took a pessimistic view of the West and the impact of its early incorporation

into the United States. Rufus King of Massachusetts
questioned Elbridge Gerry in June 1786 whether "in
true policy ought the United States to be very assiduous
to encourage their citizens to become Settlers of the
Country beyond the Apalachians." King feared the loss
of population would weaken the eastern states. "Every
emigrant to that country from the Atlantic States is
forever lost to the confederacy." He then proceeded to
give a powerful summary of the pessimists' case:

> Nature has severed the two countries by a vast and extensive
> chain of mountains; interest and convenience will keep them
> separate, and the feeble policy of our disjointed government
> will not be able to unite them. For these reasons, I have been
> opposed to encouragements of western emigrants. The States
> situated on the Atlantic are not sufficiently populous and
> loosing our Men is loosing our greatest Source of Wealth.[25]

The twin themes—that western settlement would
lead to a loss of population in the eastern states and that
the United States had too much land already—became
the stock ones for the pessimists in Congress. Paine
Wingate of New Hampshire argued that the settlement
of the West "will draw off our most valuable and enter-
prising young men and will impede the population of
our old states and prevent the establishment of manufac-
tures." Wingate elaborated the ways in which the West
would drag the country down. "I doubt," he continued,
"whether, in our day, that country will not be a damage
to us rather than an advantage. We seem to be over-
stocked with lands and I believe it had been as well for
the Indians to have kept their own territory."[26] Samuel
Meredith of Pennsylvania added another dimension to
the case against quick settlement when he argued that
an inactive American policy would prevent troublesome
and expensive tensions and wars. "It would prove a
happiness to all the settled parts of the country," he told
Thomas Fitzsimmons in November 1786, "if the Ohio
was the boundary for a number of years as well as be a
means of quieting the Indians and the Spaniards."[27]
    Even James Monroe, who later took such an energetic

part in getting the Ordinance through Congress, suc-
cumbed at times to this pessimistic assessment which, if
acted upon, would have led to no provisions for settlement and civilian government in the Northwest. In the
midst of a long letter to Thomas Jefferson in January
1786, Monroe gave his negative view of the western
issue. "I am clearly of opinion," he wrote to Jefferson,

> that to many of the most important objects of a Federal
> government, their interests [in the West] if not opposed, will
> be but little connected with ours. . . . A great part of the
> territory is miserably poor, especially that near Lake Michi-
> gan and Erie, and that upon the Mississippi and the Illinois
> consists of extensive plains which have not, and from appear-
> ances, will not have a single bush on them for ages. The
> Districts therefore within which these fall will perhaps never
> contain a sufficient number of inhabitants to entitle them to
> membership in the confederacy and in the meantime the
> people who may settle within them will be gov'd by the
> resolutions of Congress in which they will not be repre-
> sented. In many instances their interests will be opposed to
> ours.[28]

Monroe delivered himself of this pessimistic view in
January 1786, yet by April he was committed to the
more active and optimistic policy of framing a form of
government for the Northwest that would attract settlers and attach them to the Union. Monroe rejected
the pessimistic assessment because he believed that
leaving the West alone or leaving it in some dependent
connection with the confederacy would lead to the
settlers abrogating what allegiance they did have and
turning to the British. The pessimistic approach should
be rejected, Monroe explained to Jefferson, because it
"evinces plainly the policy of these men to keep them
out of the confederacy altogether. I consider this as a
dangerous, a very mischievous kind of policy calculated
to throw them into the hands of Britain."[29] In the case
of Monroe then, the evidence points clearly to a concern
for power relationships in the Old Northwest as a key
factor which convinced Monroe some sort of attractive
option would have to be presented to the settlers.

When Congress discussed the proposed ordinance in the summer of 1787, the revenue question was clearly of central importance. A successful sale of extensive western lands would help pay off some of the huge debt. William Pierce, a member of the Georgia delegation, put this consideration plainly when he wrote to William Short that "the most material business that we have lately compleated is the Government of the Western Country and the direction given to the board of Treasury to sell a large tract of the Western Lands, by which we may probably sink 4 or 5 millions of the domestic debt."[30]

But while delegates understood the revenue aspect of all this, the settlement policy was also connected with strategic circumstances in the West. Edward Carrington of Virginia summed up this important aspect of the Northwest Ordinance in a letter of 23 October 1787 to Thomas Jefferson:

> The Western Territory belonging to the United States has more effectually received the attention of Congress during this session than it ever did before. Enclosed you will receive the ordinance for establishing a Temporary government there and providing for its more easy passage into permanent state governments. Under the old arrangements the country might upon the whole have been very populous and yet be inadmissable to the rights of state government which would have been disgusting to them and ultimately inconvenient for the Empire.[31]

The theme of the supporters of the Ordinance was an optimistic one that had faith in the future of the American empire. The Ordinance would attract settlers to the United States rather than leave them to be tempted by Britain, Spain, or independence. The proposed three states would be better than a series of more numerous states because, the more states there were, the longer it would be before they could build up the population necessary for entry to the Union. If the settlers were forced to wait a long time, the Virginia delegates explained to their State Governor Edmund Randolph, "it could not be expected they would remain long contented and the Federal Government would be under the necessity of suffering them to enter into other alliances."[32]

By offering attractive terms of admission to the Union, the Ordinance would attract settlers with republican values and thus prevent the growth in the West of a heterogeneous population whose loyalty and political values would diverge from the United States. The article on the encouragement of education was framed hopefully in this connection that a literate population would appreciate the advantages of living in a republican polity. As Edmund Carrington phrased it in an almost exultant note to James Monroe on 7 August 1787, the settlement plan of the Northwest Ordinance "will be the means of introducing into the Country, in the first instance, a description of Men who will fix the character of politics throughout the whole territory and which will probably endure to the latest period of time."[33] But even as he reached this height of peroration, Carrington revealed the strategic reality behind the happy fact of republican settlement. In October 1787, he wrote to Jefferson to inform him of the first administration under the Ordinance. "The offices of the Temporary Government," he told Jefferson, "are filled up as follows: Genl. St. Clair, Govr.; Winthrop Sargent, Secretary; Genl. Parsons, Genl. Armstrong Jr. and Genl. Varnum Judges."[34] In the new settlements in this crossroads of empire, men with military experience were needed to govern.

In the fall of 1814, as he was engaged in the peace negotiations at Ghent, John Quincy Adams took stock of the relative positions of the United States and Great Britain as powers in North America. He thought that the United States' advantage in population and resources was balanced "by the great difference between the military establishments of the two Nations."[35] He developed his case by arguing that the British proposals for an Indian buffer state in the Northwest was part of a long-cherished British plan to stunt the westward expansion of American population. British naval supremacy, the much greater British military establishment in Canada, along with an Indian buffer state in the Northwest, would push the balance of forces in Britain's favor. But it was too late for such a policy to take hold. For Britain to attempt now to halt American expansion "was opposing a feather to a torrent. The population of the United States in 1810 passed 7 millions. At this time it has undoubtedly passed 8."[36] If this position in 1814 is compared to the uncertainties of 1787, when the pessimists in Congress were prepared to write-off the Northwest, then the significance of the Northwest Ordinance in strategic terms becomes manifest. Other major events played a part, especially the creation of a more effective national government by the 1787 Constitution and the purchase of Louisiana in 1803 which foreclosed the possibility of further British encroachments in the far west, but the Northwest Ordinance was the first, crucial step in an effective United States policy for the western territories. By providing attractive conditions for white settlers, by re-assuring existing and potential settlers that land titles would be solid, the 1787 Ordinance, at a critical moment for the future of power relationships in North America, tilted the balance toward the new United States.

---

1. James Monroe to John Quincy Adams, 21 July 1815, in William R. Manning, ed., *Diplomatic Correspondence of the United States. Canadian Relations 1784–1860* (Washington, D.C., 1940), 1:231 (hereafter cited as Manning, *Diplomatic Correspondence*).

2. Quoted in Edmund Morgan, *The Meaning of Independence* (New York, 1978).

3. Rhode Island Delegates to John Collins, Governor of Rhode Island, New York, 28 September 1786, in Edmund C. Burnett, *Letters of the Members of the Continental Congress* (Washington, D.C., 1936), 8:470–72 (hereafter cited as Burnett, *Letters*).

4. Jack Rakove, "Ambiguous Achievement: The Northwest Ordinance," supra, 6-7; Gordon T. Stewart, *The Origins of Canadian Politics* (Vancouver, 1986), 20; Gordon T. Stewart and G. A. Rawlyk, *The Nova Scotia Yankees and the American Revolution* (Toronto, 1972), 13–23; G. M. Craig, *Upper Canada: The Formative Years 1784–1841* (Toronto, 1963).

5. James Madison to Edmund Pendleton, New York, 24 February 1787, in Burnett, *Letters*, 547.

6. Kenneth Bourne, *Britain and the Balance of Power in North America 1815–1908* (Berkeley, 1967).

7. Thomas Jefferson to Gouverneur Morris, New York, 12 August 1790, in Manning, *Diplomatic Correspondence*, 44.

8. John Jay to John Adams, 6 September 1785, ibid., 15.

9. John Adams to John Jay, London, 15 December 1785, ibid., 339–40.

10. John Jay to Congress, 22 March 1786, ibid., 21.

11. Gouverneur Morris to George Washington, London, 17 March 1792, ibid., 393–94.

12. James Monroe to the Committee of Public Safety, 25 January 1795, ibid., 454–55.

13. John Jay to Thomas Jefferson, New York, 24 April 1787, ibid., 38.

14. John Jay to Thomas Jefferson, 14 December 1786, ibid., 32.

15. John Jay to Thomas Jefferson, 14 December 1786, ibid.

16. Edward Carrington to Edmund Randolph, Governor of Virgnia, New York, 8 December 1786, in Burnett, *Letters*, 516–18.

17. Henry Lee to George Washington, New York, 11 November 1786, ibid., 505–6.

18. Edward Rutledge to John Jay, Philadelphia, 18 August 1794, in Manning, *Diplomatic Correspondence*, 78.

19. *New York Daily Advertiser*, 23 February 1789, in Burnett, *Letters*, 824.

20. John Quincy Adams to James Monroe, 5 September 1814, in Manning, *Diplomatic Correspondence*, 652.

21. J. C. A. Stagg, *Mr. Madison's War: Politics, Diplomacy and Warfare in the Early American Republic, 1783–1830* (Princeton, 1983).

22. Albert Gallatin to James Monroe, Ghent, 20 August 1814, in Manning, *Diplomatic Correspondence*, 635–36.

23. Thomas Rodney Diary, 4 May 1786, in Burnett, *Letters*, 353.

24. Rhode Island Delegates to John Collins, New York, 28 September 1786, ibid., 470–72; Timothy Bloodworth to Richard Carwell, Governor of North Carolina, New York, 4 September 1786, ibid., 462.

25. Rufus King to Elbridge Gerry, 4 June 1786, ibid., xxix.

26. Paine Wingate to Samuel Lane, New York, 2 June 1788, ibid., 746.

27. Samuel Meredith to Thomas Fitzsimmons, November 1786, ibid., 513.

28. James Monroe to Thomas Jefferson, New York, 19 January 1786, ibid., 284–86.

29. James Monroe to Thomas Jefferson, New York, 16 July 1786, ibid., 404.

30. William Pierce to William Short, New York, 25 July 1787, ibid., 629.

31. Edward Carrington to Thomas Jefferson, New York, 23 October 1787, ibid., 660.

32. The Virginia Delegates to the Governor of Virginia, New York, 3 November 1787, ibid., 672.

33. Edward Carrington to James Monroe, New York, 7 August 1787, ibid., 631.

34. Edward Carrington to Thomas Jefferson, New York, 23 October 1787, ibid., 660.

35. John Quincy Adams, et al., to British Minister, 9 September 1814, in Manning, *Diplomatic Correspondence*, 634–35.

36. John Quincy Adams to James Monroe, Ghent, 5 September 1814, ibid., 647–48.

III

Battling Infidelity, Heathenism, and Licentiousness: New England Missions on the Post-Revolutionary Frontier, 1792–1805

RUTH H. BLOCH
Department of History, UCLA

THE NORTHWEST ORDINANCE OF 1787 SOUGHT primarily to establish a legal and political framework for the development of the West. The Ordinance had little to say about the future social and cultural life of the region other than its ambiguous comments on slavery and its tacit reinforcement of the provisions for public education already contained in the Land Ordinance of 1785. The document begged other questions about the type of society that would evolve in the territory and the basis of its cultural integration into the republic. As far as the religious future of the West was concerned, in particular, the brief statements in Articles I and III establishing religious liberty and offering general support for "religion, morality, and knowledge," provided scarcely any direction whatsoever.[1]

The most basic explanation for this silence lies, of course, in the republican belief in limited government. The experience of the Revolution had by 1787 greatly reinforced Americans' longstanding distrust of state intervention in religious life. There is, however, another, less obvious reason for the failure of the Ordinance to comment more fully on the religious future of the West. In 1787 this question simply did not seem problematic enough to address—not yet. In the Ordinance of 1785 the Continental Congress had only narrowly defeated an article setting aside government land for churches as well as for schools, and even the defeat of this measure did little to shake the assumption that American Protestantism would automatically spread to the West. The pressing questions of 1787 instead concerned the institutional structure of republican government and the basis of union among the states—questions answered in different ways during the same year by the Northwest Ordinance and the proposed United States Constitution. Other social and cultural matters related to the future settling of the West (again, with the partial exception of education and slavery) remained submerged, religion among them—either deemed irrelevant or simply taken for granted.

Among those the most complacent about the promise of western expansion in 1787 were surely orthodox New England Congregationalist clergymen. Unlike their counterparts in the southern and middle states, this group of colonial religious leaders emerged from the Revolution virtually unscathed. As early and ardent supporters of the revolutionary movement, they had fully identified with the republican cause. Despite the challenge posed to their traditional ecclesiastical order by Baptists and a few sectarians (challenges themselves hardly new), Connecticut, Massachusetts, and New Hampshire were unique among the American states in keeping their legally established, tax-supported state Congregationalist churches intact until well into the nineteenth century. Far from seeming a threat to their religious leadership, the Revolution typically appeared to Congregationalist clergymen as a harbinger of the future millennial Kingdom of God when true religion would spread across the face of the earth. Westward expansion was, in their view, a further step toward this end. Already in 1783 the Congregationalist leader Ezra Stiles preached a well-publicized Election Day sermon celebrating the prospect of New England churches "advancing forward" into the wilderness, thereby achieving a "singular superiority . . . in converting the world."[2]

The complacency of these established New England clergymen is also evident in the comparative slowness with which they organized to evangelize unchurched residents of newly settled territories. Other denominations based elsewhere in America had acted much sooner: the Anglicans and the Presbyterians beginning already during the colonial period, the Methodists increasingly in the immediate wake of the Revolution. Traditionally, however, migration from New England during the colonial period had proceeded in a gradual, orderly, and decentralized fashion, with the emigrants consistently reproducing the structure of town government and parish church organization in their new settlements.[3] Although in 1774 the Congregationalist General Association of Connecticut noted a growing need to supply preachers to the growing numbers of "destitute" unchurched settlements in the "wilderness" of northern New England, it was only with the creation of its Committee of Missions in 1792 that the Connecticut Congregationalists became the first major New England church to respond to this growing challenge in an institutionally effective manner.[4] For several years prior to that, while the post-Revolutionary emigration from southern New England to Vermont, Maine, western New York, northern Pennsylvania, and the Western Reserve in Ohio was already proceeding at record pace, the Connecticut church had simply left the employment of frontier preachers to local county associations of ministers, which had done very little.[5] Even after the creation of the Committee of Missions, the Connecticut Congregationalists can scarcely be seen as embarked on an aggressive evangelizing campaign. The number of ministers sent to unchurched areas dramatically increased between 1792 and 1798, but the policy limited these efforts to only those settlements that had issued "express applications for help."[6] And when, in 1795, the Committee encountered difficulty recruiting enough reputable, settled clergymen willing to leave their pastorates for these arduous tours, they declined to lower their ministerial standards and chose instead to cut back their operations.[7]

Despite this seeming reticence, the tone of this early missionary movement was not indifference, but optimism. The Congregational clergy was still exhilarated by its success at providing spiritual leadership during the Revolution, and saw these missions as the way simply to reinforce the preexistent Christian faith of the settlers in the new territories. Having so recently stood at the forefront of the revolutionary movement, they now dedicated themselves to consolidating the true faith of the growing republic. "So shall we behold our Jerusalem built up," declared a Connecticut minister in 1789, "this, a land of light, liberty, and religion—our country grow and increase—our empire enlarge and extend."[8] Even those early missionaries most concerned about the rugged, coarse life style of the frontier expressed a basic confidence that, in due time, Christian civilization would prevail.[9] Typically the New England missionaries of the early 1790s fully identified with the emigrants they served and regarded themselves as jointly engaged in the task of spreading a cohesive, homogenous, and orthodox New England culture over the American continent. Noting that "a large proportion of the new settlers were from New England," a missionary reporting on a 1794 tour to Genesee County, New York, confidently observed:

The inhabitants . . . retain the spirit and manner of their
native states, their reverence for the Sabbath, their zeal for
religious worship, and their decency of attendance, their
attention to literature and civilization, and their attachment
to the privileges of society. At the same time they are industrious and economical. . . . Sober, industrious, frugal citizens are the strength and glory of *States*. They have the
happiest influence on . . . civil and religious liberty and
whatever can make a nation honorable, formidable or
happy.[10]

Within a few years, however, this tone of confidence
had given way to cries of alarm. In the late 1790s
frontier settlers were repeatedly described as giving way
to the influence of "infidels," "errorists," "deists," and
"atheists."[11] The failure of New England missionaries to
convert the Indian "heathens" also suddenly received
more attention, likewise raising the question of whether
the West would be won for Christianity.[12] As a reflec-
tion of this new state of crisis, "missionary societies"
began to proliferate throughout the northeast, typically
declaring their intention to christianize both Indians
and whites in new settlements.[13] Once again, the Connecticut state church led the way with the foundation of
the Connecticut Missionary Society in 1798, an ex-
panded version of the older Committee of Missions that
now drew almost twice the financial support, included
many prominent laymen on the Board of Trustees, and
published its own magazine.[14] Between 1798 and 1801,
three more, comparable societies were formed by Massachusetts Congregationalists, and by 1807 New Hampshire, Maine, and Vermont Congregationalists had
established theirs as well. Nor were the Congregationalists alone. The Massachusetts Baptist Missionary Society was founded in 1802 and the Maine Baptist Missionary Society in 1804.[15] There were, moreover, close
relationships among these organizations. Sympathetic
reports on one another's activities indicate that even
Congregationalists and Baptists overlooked their denominational rivalry and assumed a cooperative stance.[16]
A further step toward interdenominational cooperation

was the formation of the Congregational-Presbyterian Plan of Union in 1801.

This compromising spirit is also evident in the tendency of the Connecticut Missionary Society to lower its ministerial standards. Compared to the highly reputable clergymen sent by the Committee of Missions prior to 1798, an increasing proportion were now younger and notably more obscure.[17] By 1800 the Society had abandoned the earlier requirement that missionaries be settled in their own pastorates, and even began hiring "candidates" and "licentiates" who had not yet been ordained.[18] Few efforts were now being spared in the effort to determine the religious nature of the new territories.

The sense of crisis that underlay this sudden outburst of evangelical organizing had, ironically, little to do with any sudden change within the actual religious situation in the West. To be sure, the expansion of the missionary movement was partly a delayed reaction to the continuing expansion of the unchurched population and the ever more evident religious diversity of the new settlements. The growth of Vermont Universalism, Methodism, and Free Will Baptism was especially disturbing.[19] Even in the Western Reserve, settled almost exclusively by the sons and daughters of Connecticut, Congregationalism was not keeping pace with the growing population.[20] But there is no reason to think that this situation was new in the late 1790s.

The most direct explanation for the precise timing of the surge in evangelical organization was the far more dramatic event overseas: the French Revolution. By the late 1790s New England religious opinion had swung away from initial support for the Revolution to virulent opposition, particularly in response to repeated news of the revolutionaries' public rejection of revealed Christianity. The Revolution had by then become a central issue within domestic American party politics, polarizing Jeffersonian Democratic-Republicans and Federalists. The New England established clergy was overwhelmingly Federalist. Several of the ministers who were most active in the missionary cause delivered vitriolic sermons between 1798 and 1800 loosely identifying the Republican party with a world-wide Jacobin conspiracy.[21] Virtually all of the lay leaders in the early missionary movement were also prominent figures in both local and national arch-Federalist politics.[22]

The connection in their minds between the French Revolution and the American West was basic to their newfound missionary zeal. In saving souls in the West they saw themselves as joining forces against French infidelity. This connection was rarely drawn in specifically American partisan-political terms: one Connecticut missionary's caustic observation about settlers in Vermont that "infidels in religion are apt to be Democrats"—was the exception rather than the rule.[23] Instead the connection was typically framed in universal religious terms. For these New Englanders, the institutional weakness of organized Christianity on the American frontier was one more sign of an international crisis. On the one hand, the great magnitude of events in Europe forced them to reassess their earlier patriotic assumption that the theater of world history had shifted to the New World. To sustain the ingrained belief that New England concerns possessed a global significance, these clergymen needed to determine the relationship of their own activities to the drama being enacted abroad. On the other hand, the very perception of conflict in transnational terms facilitated the identification of internal enemies. The fact that settlers were so often described as infidels, atheists, and deists—despite the fact that scarcely anyone anywhere in America at that time avowed these religious opinions—illustrates the power of this symbolic association with France. A basic doctrinal pamphlet distributed by the Missionary Society of Connecticut explained how Satan's most recent tactic in the war against Christianity was to employ the "subtil and dangerous attacks of the [French] infidel Philosophists."[24]

Just when the moral guardians of traditional New England society began to confront the difficult social and cultural problems posed by the westward movement, French social disorder and hostility toward Christianity seemed to present an object lesson on the dangers besetting a free, egalitarian, and secular state. The bloodshed and deistic religion promoted by the revolution in France and the uncontrolled expansion of the unchurched population in America were, according to their historical vision, closely linked: both revealed the strong determination of Antichrist to sabotage the faith. One Connecticut missionary commented that the main lesson taught by the French Revolution was "that Republicanism will not itself fraternize the world."[25] The only proper antidote was aggressive Christian piety. As another missionary phrased this analysis, "the gospel is the only plan of safety," the only "preservative of the world from speedy destruction."[26] "Where religion prevails," Connecticut Missionary Society trustee and Yale President Timothy Dwight agreed, "illuminatism cannot make disciples, a French directory cannot govern, a nation cannot be made slaves, nor villains, nor atheists, nor beasts."[27]

Far from provincial in their sentiments, these New Englanders derived special encouragement from the work of other missionary societies elsewhere in America and overseas. The emergent sense of world crisis sparked by the French Revolution made them particularly vocal in their support of the London Missionary Society, founded in 1795 by British Methodists, Presbyterians, Independents, and Episcopalians. When the Connecticut General Association presented its public case for the establishment of a missionary society in 1797, its "Address" contained long extracts from London Missionary Society publications. All three of the New England religious periodicals published on behalf of the missionary societies contained regular coverage of British foreign missionary activities.[28] At a time when the fledgling American republic seemed in danger of slipping into the backwaters of history, this strong sense of identification with British missionaries helped to sustain the world-wide, millennial aspirations long held by New England Protestants.[29] The fact that Protestant England had declared war on the French revolutionary government seemed to give the British a key role in accomplishing the defeat of Antichrist. Especially high hopes were aroused among the New England Congregationalists when, during the brief Peace of Amiens, the London Missionary Society launched a preliminary campaign to convert the French and Italians to the Protestant Faith.[30] Equally impressive was the geographical scope of the British missionary activity. Insofar as the New Englanders hoped for the conversion of the entire world, close identification with the British missionaries helped satisfy these global ambitions. The Constitution of the Missionary Society of Connecticut, for example, cited the success of the British missions in India, Africa, and the South Seas as "strong grounds to hope that God, in fulfillment of ancient prophecies, is about to give to his Son the Heathen for his inheritance, and the uttermost parts of the earth for his possession."[31]

It is clear that a major incentive for establishing Indian missions in the new northwestern territory lay in the New Englanders' desires to partake more fully in this international crusade. Periodic publications appeared in the religious press urging that the American societies devote more proselytising zeal to the Indians. Pressure also came from abroad. A communication from British missionaries in the East Indies, printed in the *Connecticut Evangelical Magazine,* urged the Americans to work among "the heathen" natives no matter what the difficulty or expense.[32] In 1804 the Secretary of the London Missionary Society wrote a letter to the trustees of the Connecticut Society requesting that they expand operations to "enable your Society not only to visit the vacant churches, but to extend your Christian benevolence to the native heathen."[33]

Yet the analogy between New England and British missionary activity failed to work in practice. Missions to Indians were exceptionally well-publicized but remained embarrassingly under-staffed. For all their intentions to the contrary, the New England missionaries in the West continued for many years to concentrate their attention among white settlers with New England Protestant backgrounds.[34] At most, missionaries on two- or three-month tours in the West would spend a few days preaching to a tribe in the close vicinity of the white settlements.[35] The only full-time Indian missionaries employed by any of the New England societies in this period was the Reverend David Bacon, sent by the Connecticut Society to Ottawa and Chippewa tribes along Lakes Erie and Michigan in 1800. He remained there three discouraging years, writing back periodic reports describing his various hardships and his remarkably persevering hopes for future success. At the outset Bacon's mission was the great pride of the organization, his reports conspicuously featured in the *Connecticut Evangelical Magazine.* Yet once it became clear that there would be no immediate results—that "the inheritance of the heathen" would not come right away—the trustee's initial enthusiasm subsided. Ignoring Bacon's own assessment of his situation, they abruptly decided that the mission was hopeless and transferred the disappointed Indian missionary to white settlements in the Western Reserve.[36]

Not surprisingly, letters back to the London Missionary Society assumed apologetic and defensive tones.[37] Only rarely did the New England societies defend their choice of priorities in print.[38] Insofar as their goal of converting the world required close identification with their supposed counterparts overseas, they were committed to Indian missions. The only way out of the dilemma was to insist that the settlers were as much in danger as the heathen. To make this point, they had to invoke exacting standards of institutionalized religious observance. Repeatedly, the failure regularly to observe the sabbath—by which these New Englanders meant not only collective worship but the provision of sacraments and sermons by officiating ministers—was equated with the loss of "Christianity itself."[39] In the words of the Connecticut General Association, "without the stated preaching of the word—without the ordinances of the gospel—without sanctified sabbaths, or regular religious instruction; many of them, though called Christians, are Heathen in reality."[40] Ezekiel Chapman, a missionary on the Western Reserve in 1802, recounted what he saw as the stages in an inevitable process of religious declension:

> In places where the ordinances are not administered, where the means of public religious instruction are not enjoyed, religion insensibly loses ground, and prayer in the family and closet is generally ommitted. The consequence of these things are infidelity, stupidity, and licentiousness.[41]

By thereby suggesting that the frontier settlers were on the verge of abandoning the faith, these ministers skirted the logical tension imbedded in their identification with the world missionary movement at the same time as they employed the most conservative New England standards of proper religious observation. The norms they sought to enforce involved far more than belief in Christ, individual or family prayer, and upright moral conduct. They insisted that Christianity remained essentially insecure until the time when gathered churches called settled ministers to administer regular gospel ordinances.

While claiming to counter tendencies toward apostasy, the Congregationalist missionaries always directed most of their energy toward the most receptive, if as yet unchurched, settlements. They often self-consciously concentrated their efforts on those with whom they felt the strongest social and cultural affinity. New England emigrants—typically referred to as "friends, kindred," "Brethren, children"—consistently received the most attention from these Congregationalist ministers.[42]

The missionary societies deliberately divided the frontier territory among themselves according to where most of the emigrants from their regions had settled. The Massachusetts Missionary Society sent most of its preachers to Maine, whereas the Connecticut Society decided in 1802 to concentrate its forces in "New Connecticut"—Ohio.[43] It is significant that the New England Baptist societies, in contrast, neither publicized the depravity of the frontier nor sought out their own former neighbors as much as their Congregationalist colleagues. More intent on gaining acceptance for their own denomination than on preserving an ingrained tradition of New England church polity, the Baptists evidently set far less exacting standards for religious life.[44]

In fact, throughout this early period of home mission activity, the minority denominations and sects—the Baptists, Methodists, and Universalists—appear to have been primarily bent on gaining converts in order to promote their own particular faiths.[45] The Congregationalists, to the contrary, chose to reinforce religious commitments where they were already most deeply entrenched. On the one hand, partly in order to place their provincial concerns in an international context, these New Englanders rather deceptively justified their endeavor in terms of the transatlantic missionary creed. In so doing, they drew attention to symptoms of infidelity, suggested that the settlers were somehow like heathens, and thereby claimed to promote the millennial cause of worldwide conversion. On the other hand, they maintained a sense of identification with the settlers and conceived of their mission as the transmission of the New England church order intact through the new territory.

For these orthodox New Englanders, this was always a social as well as a religious goal. Long accustomed to a parish organization which depended on religious consensus and on strong community ties, they perceived an intimate connection between religion and collective

life. To them infidelity and the westward migration both
raised the prospect of social disorganization. They
claimed over and over that Christianity offered the best
guarantee of a stable, cohesive community. Describing
the purpose of their missions, the trustees of the Connecticut Missionary Society forthrightly declared that
"the civil and political welfare of societies no less than
the present and future happiness of individuals depends
much on religious institutions."[46] Once the settlers
began to receive "the occasional ministration of proper
missionaries" these clergymen predicted that "their civil
order, every advantage of social life, and all their tempo-
ral interests, will be advanced by family order, and the
public observation of the sabbath."[47] They denied that
religious and social concerns could ever be separated,
claiming that the Bible "teaches whatever is essential to
the common weal."[48] And, in accord with their Federalist politics, their statements about society were generally conservative, both in content and in tone. They
firmly believed that public happiness depended on a
stable, unified, and hierarchical social order. This order
began, in their view, with the family, which they defined in patriarchal terms identical to those of their
Puritan forebearers. A Connecticut Missionary Society
pamphlet entitled A Summary of Christian Doctrine and
Practice: Designed Especially for the Use of People in the
New Settlements devoted several pages to the importance
of preserving the authority of husbands over wives,
parents over children, masters over servants. Beyond
the family, the class status of "superiors" over their social
"inferiors" won missionary endorsement as well.[49]

While assuming that good societies have fixed and
layered structures, however, these evangelicals also
firmly believed that status should accrue to virtue as well
as to wealth. In their view, prestige should reward dis-
creet, steadfast, pious and socially responsible men. In
accord with this notion of an honorable and dependable
elite, they despised acquisitiveness and generally mis-
trusted new wealth. They especially deplored the fact

that economic opportunity in the West often brought
men of doubtful character into positions of leadership—
such as "the great land dealers" who refused to support a
ministry in the new settlements.[50] The qualities they
admired the most in individuals were "chastity, tem-
perance, and sobriety."[51] They proudly characterized
their own supporters on the frontier—the influential
and the more modest alike—as "respectable," "judi-
cious, steady, and serious."[52]

Infidels, by contrast, were portrayed as undermining
not only Christian belief but family order and social
responsibility. They were described as "licentious," as
interested only in the "gratification of their lusts and
passions."[53] Among such degenerate characters, "self-
love is to be indulged to the highest degree; covetous-
ness also is to reign uncontrolled; boasting is to be free
in everyone's mouth; pride is to have its full run."[54]
Once "you drive religion from a people," the former
missionary William Lyman ominously observed, "you
present to the view of degraded man the groveling scene
of a lustful paradise."[55] Society needed religion to curb
such destructive individual impulses and to instill a
spirit of mutual responsibility for family and community. Nor were outright infidels the only problem. Almost as dangerous were the various "false teachers,"
"deluded religionists," and "self-styled preachers of the
gospel" active in their missionary fields.[56] Most of these
contemptible characters, usually beneath the dignity of
being referred to by creed, appear to have been those
"perfectly selfish" Arminians—the Methodists and the
Universalists—who, by rejecting the Calvinist doctrine of predestination, promoted the individualistic
view that sinners could transform themselves and effect
their own salvation.[57] Fearful that frontier society
might never properly congeal, these Congregationalist
Calvinists stressed "the salutary tendency of the Missionary Societies to reform selfish man."[58]

It was these anti-individualistic social values, together with the sense of international crisis, that gave

rise to New England evangelical activism in the West at
the turn of the century. As far as their actual effects
were concerned, by any objective measure, the missions
fell far short of their original goal. The New England
Congregational Church was, in the words of religious
historian William Warren Sweet, unable to retain "the
allegiance of a fair proportion of her children on the
frontier."[59] The missionaries left in their wake no homogenous religious order, no end to individual selfish-
ness. Yet already by 1805 the missionary societies were
over-flowing with self-congratulations. As a publication
of the Connecticut society boasted, its "good effects
. . . in the new settlements [have been] beyond calcula-
tion. . . . The gospel has been preached and the ordinances delivered through a vast tract of country. . . .
Through the grace of God and the instrumentality of
our missionaries, the wilderness and the solitary place
have been made glad and the desert hath blossomed as
the rose."[60]

How can we explain this newfound satisfaction? It
was in part the consequence of the spread of religious
revivalism—the beginnings of the Second Great Awakening—which New England missionaries in the West
had, indeed, helped to promote. New England had
experienced its own wave of revivals starting in 1797,
and by 1803 the Great Kentucky Revival had spread
northward into the missionary fields of western Pennsylvania and the Western Reserve.[61] Despite some missionaries' misgivings about the strange noises, trances,
trembling, and fainting characteristic of the western
revival, they welcomed the awakenings and vigorously
defended their authenticity.[62] Within a few years many
churches were gathered and ministers settled in them—
so many, that after 1807 the Missionary Society of
Connecticut began to recruit indigenous clergymen
rather than relying on easterners willing to go west.[63]

In addition, and perhaps more importantly, the exu-
berant mood of the New England evangelicals reflected
their own change of attitude. Their very worst fears

had, after all, proved unjustified. The French Revolution had wound its way away from Jacobinism to the far less threatening Napoleonic state. Domestically, the election of Jefferson to the Presidency had not, in fact, led to an onslaught of infidelity. Moreover, I want to suggest, the very experience of the frontier missions had brought them to accept the facts of political and religious heterogeneity and competition. It may even be that the western missions had a greater effect on New England religious attitudes than they had on the religion of the new territory. In 1803, the same Connecticut missionary who had in 1799 equated infidelity and Jeffersonianism wrote from northern Pennsylvania generously conceding that "most of the ministers and serious people in this part of the country, and of all classes, are Democrats."[64] Two years later he similarly acknowledged that "most of the serious people" in a certain Ohio community were Baptists and Methodists, and even protested that some of his Presbyterian colleagues held "too much bitterness against opposite denominations."[65]

On the one hand, the spirit of rivalry between Congregationalists and Baptists grew more intense as both denominations gave up the earlier goal of Calvinist unity and turned more to the pursuit of purely denominational ends.[66] Among the Congregationalists, previously anonymous "errorists" or "false teachers" now increasingly became duly labeled as Baptists, Methodists, and Universalists.[67] Yet, on the other hand, the very acceptance of this interdenominational competition reflected a tacit abandonment of their original plan of spreading the New England ecclesiastical order across the American continent.

This change in attitude toward the future of the West can be seen as the religious dimension of the so-called "Revolution of 1800." For the established New England churches, it was more of a Revolution than the American Revolution itself. For the experience of evangelizing the frontier in the period 1797-1805, combined with

European and domestic political developments, finally brought them to embrace the principle of voluntary religious association.[68]

Not that the New England clergy entirely gave up the goal of exerting a dominant influence over the society of the new territories. Virtually all that remained of their former ideal of a religiously unified, organic social order was, however, a residual elitism. Long accustomed to boasting that the "first," "eminent," "wealthy and leading characters" in the settlements offered them the most encouragement, Plan of Union missionaries in the early nineteenth century continued to draw attention to their distinctively elite following.[69] But this very emphasis on their upper-class constituency, while certainly conservative to our modern ears, stemmed from their newfound, liberal acceptance of social and religious diversity in America. For them it was a diversity that was still, of course, confined within white Protestantism. Only later would the evangelical movement face the deeper challenges of abolitionism, Indian warfare, and Catholic immigration—challenges it was prepared only partly to meet.

---

1. "Northwest Ordinance, July 13, 1787," in Richard B. Morris, ed., *Basic Documents on the Confederation and Constitution* (New York, 1970), 128–29.

2. Ezra Stiles, *The United States Elevated to Glory and Honour* (New Haven, 1783), 57. Also see Thomas Wells Bray, *A Dissertation on the Sixth Vial* (Hartford, 1780), 75–76; Ammi Ruhamah Robbins, *The Empires and Dominions of the World* (Hartford, 1789), 23, 39. On millennial ideas within the Revolutionary movement, see Ruth H. Bloch, *Visionary Republic: Millennial Themes in American Thought, 1756–1800* (New York, 1985).

3. Colin B. Goodykoontz, *Home Missions on the American Frontier* (Caldwell, Idaho, 1939); Oliver Wendell Elsbree, *The Rise of the Missionary Spirit* (Williamsport, Penn., 1928); Lois Wendland Banner, "The Protestant Crusade: Religious Missions, Benevolence, and Reform in the United States" (Ph.D. diss., Columbia University, 1970).

4. Quotations from Edwin Pond Palmer, *Historical Discourse in Commemoration of the One Hundredth Anniversary of the Missionary Society of Connecticut* (Hartford, 1929), 7.

5. Lois Kimball Mathews, *The Expansion of New England* (Boston, 1909), 174-76; Charles Roy Keller, *The Second Great Awakening in Connecticut* (New Haven, 1942); Cong. Ch. in Conn., *A Narrative of the Missions to the New Settlements* (New Haven, 1794), 1.

6. Cong. Ch. in Conn., *Address to the Inhabitants of the New Settlements in the Northern and Western Parts of the United States* (New Haven, 1793), 3.

7. Cong. Ch. in Conn., *A Continuation of the Narrative of the Missions to the New Settlements* (New Haven, 1795), 11.

8. Robbins, *Empires and Dominions*, 39.

9. For example, Nathan Perkins, *A Narrative of a Tour through the State of Vermont from April 27 to June 12, 1789*, 3d ed. (Woodstock, Vt., 1937), 18–19.

10. Cong. Ch. in Conn., *A Narrative of Missions* (New Haven, 1794), 15.

11. For example: Cong. Ch. in Conn., *A Continuation of the Narrative* (New Haven, 1797), 8; Miss. Soc. of Conn., *A Second Address from the Trustees of the Missionary Society. . .and a Narrative on the Subject of Missions* (Hartford, 1801), 5–6; Miss. Soc. of Conn., *A Narrative on the Subject of Missions* (Hartford, 1802), 6–9; *Connecticut Evangelical Magazine* 1 (March 1801): 324; *Connecticut Evangelical Magazine* 3 (November 1802): 194–95; Nathaneal Emmons, *A Sermon, Delivered Before the Massachusetts Missionary Society. . .May 27, 1800* (Charlestown, Mass., 1800), 26; *Massachusetts Missionary Magazine* 1 (1803): 8.

12. Cong. Ch. in Conn., *An Address of the General Association of Connecticut, to the District Associations* (Norwich, 1797), 7.

13. Elsbree, *Rise of Missionary Spirit*, 60–80; *Connecticut Evangelical Magazine* 1 (July 1800): 13–14 and 5 (July 1804): 33; *Massachusetts Missionary Magazine* 1 (1803): 5–6, 76. Among the Congregationalists, the Rhode Island Missionary Society was exceptional in its focus on Afro-Americans rather than Indians. The Constitution of the Massachusetts Baptist Society also withheld formal commitment to preach to the Indians. See the *Massachusetts Baptist Missionary Magazine* 1 (September 1803): 6.

14. According to the "Funds" section of the Society's annual *Narratives*, they leapt from approximately $1,000 to $2,000.

15. Elsbree, *Rise of Missionary Spirit*, 60–68.

16. For an example of the close alliance between Congregationalist and Baptist missionaries, see "The Diaries of the Rev. Seth Williston, D.D., 1796–1800," J. Q. Adams, ed., in *Journal of the Presbyterian Historical Society*, 10 (1919–20): 30, 33. Another sign of this cooperation was the interdenominational auxiliary organization, the Boston Female Society for Missionary Purposes, founded in 1800.

17. In 1793–97 the median age of Connecticut missionaries was 48 years, whereas from 1798–1804 it dropped to 30 years. Similarly, among the latter group 22% were too little known to leave biographical information (compared to 15% in the earlier group), and only 88% of those whose basic biographies are known (compared to 100%) attended college. This evidence is from my biographical study of eighty-nine missionaries of the Connecticut Society, based primarily on the Society's annual *Narratives of the Missions* (1793–1810); *Connecticut Evangelical Magazine*; William B. Sprague, *Annals of the American Pulpit* (New York, 1857), vols. 1–4;

Sprague, *Annals of the American Pulpit* (New York, 1857), vols. 1–4; Franklin B. Dexter, *Biographical Sketches of the Graduates of Yale College* (New York, 1903-1911), vols. 2–5; William S. Kennedy, *The Plan of Union: Or a History of the Presbyterian and Congregational Churches of the Western Reserve* (Hudson, Ohio, 1856).

18. In the 1793–97 group, 94% were both ordained and settled, whereas in the 1798–1804 group only 19% were both ordained and settled; 30% were unsettled and ordained; and 44% were both unsettled and unordained. For sources, see note 17 above.

19. David M. Ludlum, *Social Ferment in Vermont, 1791–1850*, 2d ed. (New York, 1939), 34–37.

20. William Warren Sweet, *Religion on the American Frontier* (Chicago, 1939), 3:14.

21. See, for example, Timothy Dwight, *The Duty of Americans, at the Present Crisis* (New Haven, 1798); Levi Hart, *Religious Improvements of the Death of Great Men* (Norwich, 1800); Chauncy Lee, *The Tree of Knowledge of Political Good and Evil* (Bennington, Vt., 1800); Cyprian Strong, *Connecticut Election Sermon, May 9, 1799* (Hartford, 1799).

22. Eight of the ten lay trustees of the Connecticut Missionary Society between 1798 and 1810, for example, fit this description. They were John Treadwell, lieutenant governor of Connecticut; Jonathan Brace, congressman, judge and mayor of Hartford; Roger Newberry, assemblyman; John Davenport, congressman and prominant lawyer; Andrew Kingsbury, state treasurer and founder of Hartford Bank; John Porter, state comptroller; Aaron Austin, Connecticut councilman; Jedidiah Huntington, general and president of Union Bank; Oliver Ellsworth, retired chief justice of the U.S. Supreme Court; and Asher Miller, mayor of Middletown, councilman, and judge. This information is from the *Dictionary of American Biography*; Dexter, *Sketches of Yale Graduates*; Richard J. Purcell, *Connecticut in Transition* (Washington, D.C., 1918).

23. Thomas Robbins, *Diary of Thomas Robbins, D.D., 1796–1854* (Boston, 1886), 1:84. Most standard accounts of the evangelical movement in New England portray it as a direct expression of the clergy's antidemocratic Federalist social and political beliefs. See, for example: Charles I. Foster, *An Errand of Mercy: The Evangelical United Front, 1790–1837* (Chapel Hill, 1960); Clifford S. Griffin, *Their Brothers' Keepers: Moral Stewardship in the United States, 1800–1865* (New Brunswick, 1960); and John R. Bodo, *The Protestant Clergy and Public Issues, 1812–1848* (Princeton, 1954). Interpretations more similar to mine are: Lois W. Banner, "Religious Benevolence as Social Control: A Critique of an Interpretation," *Journal of American History*, 60 (June 1973): 23–41; Donald M. Scott, *From Office to Profession: The New England Ministry, 1750–1850* (Philadelphia, 1978).

24. Miss. Soc. of Conn., *A Summary of Christian Doctrine and Practice: Designed Especially for the Use of People in the New Settlements* (Hartford, 1804), 10.

25. Seth Williston, "The Diaries of the Rev. Seth Williston, D.D., 1796–1800," J. Q. Adams, ed., in *Journal of the Presbyterian Historical Society* 9 (1917–1918): 34.

26. Alexander Gillet, "True Christianity the Safety of this World," in *Sermons on Important Subjects* (Hartford, 1797), 462.

27. Dwight, *Duty*, 18.

28. The *Connecticut Missionary Magazine*, the *Massachusetts Missionary Magazine*, and the *Massachusetts Baptist Missionary Magazine* all published some news of British missions nearly every issue.

29. For the background of millennial thought, see Bloch, *Visionary Republic*.

30. See, for example, *Interesting Account of Religion in France* (New York, 1803), a pamphlet published under the auspices of the Connecticut Missionary Society.

31. Miss. Soc. of Conn., *The Constitution of the Missionary Society of Connecticut* (Hartford, 1800), 14.

32. *Connecticut Evangelical Magazine* 2 (October 1801): 156–59.

33. *Connecticut Evangelical Magazine* 4 (January 1804): 277.

34. *Connecticut Evangelical Magazine* 1 (July 1800): 5; 1 (March 1801): 321–22; 4 (July 1803): 27–31; 5 (November 1804): 180–82; 6 (December 1805): 227.

35. For example, *Connecticut Evangelical Magazine* 6 (November 1805): 174–75; *Massachusetts Baptist Missionary Magazine* 2 (December 1808): 114–18.

36. Leonard Bacon, *Sketch of the Rev. David Bacon* (Boston, 1876). According to David Bacon's son Leonard, the trustees withdrew their support because they claimed to be unable to shoulder the expense; yet, by 1802 they were collecting more than enough in interest alone from the Society's accumulating "permanent fund," ibid., 74; Miss. Soc. of Conn., *Narrative on the Subject of Missions. . .* (Hartford, 1802), 16–19.

37. For example, Letters of April 20, 1803 and May 4, 1804 from Trustees of the Missionary Society of Connecticut to the London Missionary Society (Archives of the London Missionary Society, London). I am indebted to Henry F. May for sharing his notes from this archive.

38. For example, Miss. Soc. of Conn., *A Summary of Christian Doctrine*, 48.

39. Cong. Ch. in Conn., *A Continuation of the Narrative of the Missions* (New Haven, 1797), 12; Amos Basset, "Missionary Sermon," *Connecticut Evangelical Magazine* 5 (August 1804): 42.

40. Cong. Ch. in Conn., *An Address of the General Association of Connecticut, to the District Associations (Norwich, 1797)*; *Connecticut Evangelical Magazine* 3 (November 1802): 194–95.

41. Miss. Soc. of Conn., *An Act to Incorporate the Trustees* (Hartford, 1802), 8.

42. Cong. Ch. in Conn., *A Continuation of the Narrative of the Missions*, 7, 12; *Massachusetts Missionary Magazine* 3 (March 1806): 384–85; Nathan Strong, *A Sermon at the Ordination of the Rev. Thomas Robbins* (Hartford, 1803), 9.

43. Miss. Soc. of Conn., *Narrative on the Subject of Missions* (Hartford, 1802), 13.

44. Cf. the missionary reports in the *Massachusetts Baptist Missionary Magazine*, 1, 2 (September 1803, December 1809).

45. Lois Banner, "Religious Benevolence as Social Control" and "The Protestant Crusade." Banner, however, exaggerates the importance of the denominational interests of the Congregationalists, seeing their mission as not "successful" because they concentrated on their own kind. "Protestant Crusade," 28–32.

46. Miss. Soc. of Conn., *Address to the People of the State of Connecticut* (Hartford, 1801), 13–14; Miss. Soc. of Conn., *Constitution*, 3.

47. Miss. Soc. of Conn., *A Continuation of the Narrative*, 13–14.

48. Miss. Soc. of Conn., *Summary of Christian Doctrine*, 51.

49. Ibid., 51–54.

50. *Connecticut Evangelical Magazine* 1 (March 1801): 324; Timothy Dwight, *Travels in New England and New York*, ed. Barbara M. Solomon, 4 vols. (Cambridge, Mass., 1969), 2:163.

51. Miss. Soc. of Conn., *Summary of Christian Doctrine*, 48–50.

52. For example, *Connecticut Evangelical Magazine* 2 (September 1801): 118; Miss. Soc. of Conn., *Narrative on the Subject of Missions* (Hartford, 1802), 12; Miss. Soc. of Conn., *Narrative on the Subject of Missions* (Hartford, 1806), 5.

53. "Thoughts on Infidelity," *Connecticut Evangelical Magazine* 1 (October 1800): 129–31.

54. *Connecticut Evangelical Magazine* 1 (February 1801): 295.

55. William Lyman, *The Happy Nation* (Hartford, 1806), 28.

56. For example, Miss. Soc. of Conn., *Address to the People of Connecticut* (Hartford, 1801), 5–6; *Connecticut Evangelical Magazine* 2 (February 1802): 313; Miss. Soc. of Conn., *Narrative on the Subject of Missions* (Hartford, 1809), 7, 10, 11; Miss. Soc. of Conn., *Narrative on the Subject of Missions* (Hartford, 1810), 10; Dwight, *Travels in New England* 2:162–63.

57. Seth Williston, "Diaries," 9:383.

58. Miss. Soc. of Conn., *An Act to Incorporate the Trustees* (Hartford, 1803), 14.

59. Sweet, *Religion on the American Frontier*, 3:14.

60. Miss. Soc. of Conn., *Narrative on the Subject of Missions* (Hartford, 1805), 4. Also see, for example, *Connecticut Evangelical Magazine* 2 (November 1801): 176–77; *Massachusetts Missionary Magazine* 3 (June 1805): 3; "Report of the Trustees of the Hampshire Missionary Society," *Connecticut Evangelical Magazine* 7 (March 1807): 355.

61. Keller, *Second Great Awakening*, 3; Catharine C. Cleaveland, *The Great Revival in the West, 1797–1805* (Chicago, 1916), 83–85.

62. *Connecticut Evangelical Magazine* 1 (August 1800): 77; 1 (October 1800): 157; 1 (February 1801): 286–91; 2 (July 1801): 27; 2 (September 1801): 104–5; 2 (November 1801): 176–77, 198; 2 (March 1802): 354–60; 2 (April 1802), 392–93; 2 (May 1802): 430; 2 (June 1802): 477; 3 (August 1802): 68; 3 (October 1802): 121–26; 3 (November 1802): 182–88; 3 (February 1803): 315, 319; 4 (September 1803): 114; Miss. Soc. of Conn., *Constitution*, 12–14; Miss. Soc. of Conn., *Narrative on the Subject of Missions* (Hartford, 1804), 7; Thomas Robbins, *Diary*, 1:211–15, 221, 263; Joseph Badger, *A Memoir of Rev. Joseph Badger; Containing an Autobiography, and Selections from his Private Journal and Correspondence* (Hudson, Ohio, 1851), 44, 50, 52, 64–65, 85.

63. Miss. Soc. of Conn., *Address from the Trustees . . . to the Ministers and People* (Hartford, 1807); Miss. Soc. of Conn., *Narrative on the Subject of Missions* (Hartford, 1809). According to my own investigation of missionary biographies, 24% of those hired by the Connecticut Missionary Society in the period 1805–1810 already lived in the new settlements, compared to 4% in the period 1798–1804. For sources, see note 17 above.

64. Robbins, *Diary*, 1:21.

65. Ibid., 253, 267. His changing attitude toward Baptists and Methodists can be traced in the entries on pp. 90, 207, 214, 223–24, and 285.

66. For Baptists, see the *Massachusetts Baptist Missionary Magazine* 1 (January 1802): 376; 2 (1808): 38–39; 2 (September 1809): 201–2; 2 (May 1809): 164–65.

67. For example, Jacob Cram, *Journal of a Missionary Tour* (Rochester, 1809); John F. Schermerhorn and Samuel J. Mills, *A Correct View of That Part of the United States which lies West of the Alleghany Mountains* (Hartford, 1814); Samuel J. Mills and Daniel Smith, *Report of a Missionary Tour through that Part of the United States which lies West of the Alleghany Mountains* (Andover, Mass., 1815).

68. Without concentrating on the early western experience, Donald Scott's *From Office to Profession* makes a similar argument.

69. For example, *Connecticut Evangelical Magazine* 2 (1801): 235; Cong. Ch. in Conn., *Narrative of the Missions* (New Haven, 1794), 13–14; Miss. Soc. of Conn., *Address to the People* (Hartford, 1801), 6; Cram, *Journal,* esp. 35; Schermerhorn and Mills, *A Correct View*; Mills and Smith, *Report of a Missionary Tour.*.

IV

Slavery and Bondage in the "Empire of Liberty"

PAUL FINKELMAN
Department of History University Center at
Binghamton, SUNY Binghamton, New York

THE RELATIONSHIP BETWEEN THE NORTHWEST
Ordinance and slavery is paradoxical.[1] The Ordinance
appeared to prohibit human bondage in its famous Article VI, which declared:

> That there shall be neither slavery nor involuntary servitude
> in the said territory otherwise than in the punishment of
> crimes whereof the party shall have been duly convicted:
> *Provided, always,* That any person escaping into the same,
> from whom labor or service is lawfully claimed by any one of
> the original States, such fugitive may be lawfully reclaimed
> and conveyed to the person claiming his or her labor or
> service as aforesaid.

Despite this provision, slavery was a vigorous institution in the western portions of the Territory. From 1788
until 1807 residents frequently petitioned Congress to
allow some form of slaveholding. Territorial governors,
such as Arthur St. Clair and William Henry Harrison
were frankly opposed to any strict implementation of
Article VI. In the absence of Congressional action,
territorial legislatures in Indiana and Illinois adopted
slave codes based on the laws of Virginia. Statehood

changed little for bondsmen and bondswomen living in some parts of the region. Slaves were held in Indiana through the 1830s and the institution did not disappear from Illinois until 1848. At the bicentennial of the Ordinance it is clear that Article VI failed to end slavery immediately in the Northwest. On the other hand, it is also apparent that in the long run the Ordinance helped put slavery on the road to ultimate extinction in the area north of the Ohio River.

For antebellum northerners the significance of the Ordinance was less ambiguous. A young Salmon P. Chase writing as if the Ordinance were a sacred text, called it "a pillar of cloud by day, and of fire by night, in the settlement of the northwestern states." This "last gift of the congress of the old confederation to the country" contained "the true theory of American liberty." Alluding to the many protections for slavery in the Constitution, Chase proudly noted that the Ordinance affirmed the "genuine principles of freedom, unadulterated by that compromise with circumstances, the effects of which are visible in the constitution and history of the union." To an aging Edward Coles, the antislavery former governor of Illinois, Article VI appeared "marvelous" and showed "the profound wisdom of those who framed such an efficacious measure for our country." Coles contrasted the sectional tension following the Kansas-Nebraska Act to an earlier period when "the Territories subject to it [the Ordinance] were quiet, happy, and prosperous." Coles believed that if American politicians had followed the pattern set by the Ordinance the turmoil of the 1850s might have been avoided. Abraham Lincoln agreed. In his attacks on popular sovereignty, Lincoln pointed to the history of the Ordinance. Comparing the slave state of Kentucky to the free states of the Northwest, Lincoln asked "What made the difference? Was it climate? No!. . . Was it soil? No!" He declared it was the Ordinance which kept slavery out of the Northwest. For men like Chase, Coles, and Lincoln the Ordinance was responsible for the creation of the free states along the Ohio River.[2]

I. An Ambiguous Article

How do we balance the nineteenth-century reverence for the Ordinance in general, and Article VI in particular, with a twentieth-century understanding of how limited the Article was? A careful examination of the adoption of the Ordinance suggests that Article VI was haphazardly drafted and barely debated. The intentions of its framers were ambiguous at best. At the time of its passage the Ordinance did not threaten slavery in the South, and may even have strengthened it there. Nor did the Ordinance immediately or directly affect slavery in the territory north of the Ohio River. Slavery continued for decades in the region. Thus in the nineteenth-century usage of the term, the Ordinance was not abolitionist and barely "antislavery."

It is unlikely that all those who voted for the Ordinance thought Article VI was antislavery. The congressmen from the Deep South who voted for the Ordinance were not consciously undermining slavery. On the contrary, the slaveholders who voted for the Ordinance may have believed that Article VI actually strengthened slavery. In 1784 Congress had rejected an attempt to prohibit slavery in *all* the western territories. Because the 1787 Ordinance only governed the northern territories, Southerners probably believed that the Ordinance implied that the territories south of the Ohio River were open to slavery.[3] Furthermore, the Ordinance's fugitive slave clause offered protection to slaveowners whose property might escape into the Territory. Since the Articles of Confederation contained no such protection, and the Constitutional Convention had not yet added a similar clause to the proposed new compact, this was an important gain for slaveowners.[4]

While the Ordinance gave support to slavery in the

South, it did not destroy slavery north of the Ohio. Article VI was not an emancipation proclamation for the Northwest. No slaves were freed immediately because of the Ordinance. Neither the Ordinance nor the state constitutions of the free states in the Northwest led to an immediate end to slavery throughout the area, although in the long run the Article helped set the stage for the emergence of five free states in the region.[5]

An examination of the transition from slavery to liberty in the Northwest illustrates the ambivalence of the founding generation over slavery, the naïveté of the early opponents of the peculiar institution, the tenacity of slave owners in maintaining control over their "servants," even when they lived in theoretically "free" jurisdictions, and the support for slavery expansion that existed in the early national period.[6] Finally, this examination illustrates the difficulty of ending a powerful institution merely by constitutional dictates and without the support of legislative enactments and executive enforcement.

The failure of the Ordinance and state constitutions to end slavery immediately has a fourfold explanation. First, Article VI was drafted quickly and accepted without debate. Such debate might have clarified its meaning. After Article VI was added the rest of the Ordinance was not altered to provide internal consistency in the document. As a result the specific dictates of the Ordinance protected some slavery in the area. For example, throughout the Ordinance there are references to "free" inhabitants of the Territory, indicating that "unfree" inhabitants might also be allowed to live there.

Second, slavery had a certain staying power—a power of inertia—which made its eradication difficult. Slavery existed in the Northwest before the Ordinance was enacted, and the mere passage of a law by a distant and virtually powerless Congress could hardly effect immediate change, nor would a state constitution necessarily end slavery immediately. Notions of private property fundamental to the ideology of the American

Revolution further strengthened existing slavery in the Territory. Was it fair, asked men raised on Lockean concepts of "life, liberty, and property," to deprive one man of his property to give another his liberty? For example, in 1815 Pennsylvania's Chief Justice William Tilghman concluded that property was as important as liberty. In denying the freedom claim of the slave Peggy, he wrote: "I know that freedom is to be favoured, but we have no right to favour it at the expense of property." Tilghman articulated an attitude prevalent throughout the legal community. Perhaps it is not surprising, therefore, that the Illinois Constitution of 1818 protected slavery and involuntary servitude and that until 1845 the Illinois Supreme Court was unwilling to free all the slaves (or their descendants) in that state. [7]

Third, the abolition of slavery in the Northwest Territory created serious conflict-of-laws questions. The three most important antebellum states in the area—Ohio, Indiana, and Illinois—shared long borders with slave states. These borders were demarcated by the two great river highways of the American interior, the Ohio and the Mississippi. Numerous masters traveling with their slaves on these waterways found it necessary or convenient to land on the free side of these rivers. In later years the national road would begin in the slave state of Maryland, but pass through three of the Northwestern states. If these states did not allow transit with slaves then comity between the states and harmony within the Union would be disrupted. On the other hand, to allow such transit would require the states to violate their own constitutional prohibitions of slavery. This was so because even slaves temporarily in a free state were, nevertheless, slaves. As lawyers in England had successfully argued in Somerset v Stewart, and as antislavery lawyers and politicians would argue in the antebellum period, freedom was essentially indivisible. It was impossible to bring slaves into a free jurisdiction without bringing some or all of the attributes of a system of slavery with them. If the slave followed the master into a free territory or state, so would the whip, the chain, and the coercion of the master.[8]

Finally, there was a lack of will on the part of many local officials, as well as officials of the national government, to actually enforce the spirit, and perhaps the precise letter, of the Ordinance. Even those opposed to slavery, or ambivalent about it, were willing to allow the institution to survive in the Northwest on the theory that the diffusion of slaves throughout the nation would benefit both the slaves and the white population. This theory was supported by many slaveholding settlers in the territory who were also not anxious to see the Ordinance implemented.

II. The Northwest Ordinance

On its face, the language of Article VI appears to be straightforward and conclusive. The words "there shall be neither slavery nor involuntary servitude" seem to mean that all slavery is prohibited in the Territory and that the status of "slave" cannot be recognized by the laws of the Territory. Yet, this apparently conclusive language was undermined by the fugitive slave provision of the Article. The Article gives no hint as to how a fugitive slave was to be treated in the Territory. Could a master beat his fugitive with impunity? Might a master rape his female fugitive slave? What would be the status of the child of a fugitive born in the Territory? These questions, and similar ones, suggest that slavery presented problems which might not be easily overcome by a single article in the Ordinance.

The apparent simplicity of Article VI is further undermined by other provisions of the Ordinance and by the circumstances of the drafting of Article VI itself. The Ordinance initially consisted of fourteen sections which outlined how the territory was to be governed, and five "articles" which would "forever remain unalterable, unless by common consent."[9] This proposed

Ordinance, with no mention of slavery, was discussed intermittently between May 1786 and May 1787. In April and May 1787 the Ordinance received two favorable readings in the Congress. A third reading, set for May 10, was postponed, and by May 12 the Congress lacked a quorum. When Congress resumed its deliberations in July a new committee was formed to finish work on the Ordinance. On July 11 that committee reported the Ordinance, which did not contain the slavery clause. On the 12th the Ordinance went through a second reading and was scheduled for a final vote the next day. Again, no mention of slavery was made in the Ordinance or on the floor of the Congress. On July 13 Nathan Dane, a delegate from Massachusetts, proposed the addition of Article VI. This amendment was apparently accepted without debate or protest. The Ordinance, with the slavery prohibition now added to it, passed by a unanimous vote of all the states present.[10]

This chain of events remains a puzzle. Although Nathan Dane drafted Article VI in committee, historians have long disputed whether or not he deserved credit for the famous provision. While that debate remains unresolved is it also not as compelling as the questions surrounding why the southern majority then in the Congress so readily accepted the clause.[11] Staughton Lynd offered three major explanations: that southerners expected the Northwest to be sympathetic to southern issues even if it had no slaves; that the Northwest Ordinance tacitly implied that the southwest would remain open to slavery; and that Article VI was part of a larger compromise which included the final adoption of the three-fifths clause by the Constitutional Convention.[12] More recently Peter Onuf has endorsed the first two of these explanations.[13] I, too, endorse the first two explanations, but, as I explain below, I find the third unconvincing.

The notion that the Ordinance implied that the territory south of the Ohio would remain open to slavery is also supported by an economic explanation of southern support for the Ordinance first offered by Congressman William Grayson of Virginia. Shortly after the Ordinance passed, Grayson explained to James Monroe that Article VI "was agreed to by the Southern members for the purpose of preventing Tobacco and Indigo from being made" in the Northwest. The Ordinance would thus prevent the Northwest from competing with the emerging Southwest. The fugitive slave clause in Article VI doubtless helped gain the votes of southerners, and may have in fact been the necessary element in obtaining their support for the ban on slavery.[14]

Another possible reason for southern support of the article prohibiting slavery was the need to pass an Ordinance that would satisfy Manassah Cutler, the lobbyist for the New England investors who formed the Ohio Land Company.

The immediate impetus for passage of the Ordinance, for both southern and northern congressmen, was the possibility of selling some five million acres of land to Cutler and his associates. Immediately after passage of the Ordinance, Virginia's Richard Henry Lee told his correspondents that the Ordinance was passed as "preparatory to the sale of that Country [Ohio]." Lee noted that as soon as the Ordinance was passed Congress considered "a proposition made for the purchase of 5 or 6 millions of Acres, in order to lessen the domestic debt."[15] Evidence of this sort led the nineteenth century historian William F. Poole to conclude that the "chief motive of the Southern members in voting unanimously for the Ordinance was doubtless to relieve the financial embarrassment of the government, and to bring the public lands into the market at the highest price." Poole further argued that the slavery prohibition was placed in the Ordinance at the insistence of Manasseh Cutler, because Congress felt it must frame "an instrument which would be satisfactory to the party proposing to purchase these lands."[16] Perhaps informed by the realities of Gilded Age politics, Poole saw the lobbyist for the land company as the most important actor on the scene.

Cutler came to New York on July 6 to lobby for the right to purchase land for the Ohio Company. On the 10th he presented some suggestions for amendments to the Ordinance to the committee and then immediately left New York for Philadelphia. On the 13th Congress adopted the Ordinance, with the slavery prohibition.[17] It is unknown whether Cutler would have agreed to purchase Ohio lands had the Ordinance not contained the prohibition of slavery. His known antipathy to slavery suggests that he was instrumental in persuading the committee, and the Congress, to accept the clause.[18] On the other hand, he apparently was willing to accept the version of the Ordinance he read on July 10, which did not include the slavery prohibition, because he left New York immediately after giving his suggested amendments to the committee. Had he been overwhelmingly concerned with the fate of his suggestions Cutler would probably have stayed in New York for the vote on the thirteenth.

It is impossible to know whether Cutler's proposed amendments even included the prohibition of slavery, but there is no convincing evidence that they did. Cutler's diary entry on this subject does not indicate what the amendments were. We might assume that had he written the slavery prohibition he would have noted it in his diary. Men who keep diaries do not, after all, usually forget to write down when they are instrumental in a momentous historical event. Moreover, the best evidence for Cutler's authorship is suspect. It comes, not from Cutler himself, but from the filiopietistic claims of his son, who recalled after Cutler's death that his father had personally claimed to have authored Article VI. Cutler himself left no written documentation to support this claim. Even his presence in New York is ambiguous. He arrived on July 6, wrote down some suggested amendments to the pending bill, and left on the 10th. On the 11th, after Cutler had left New York, the bill, as read in Congress, did not contain Article VI. Not until the 13th, after Cutler was in Philadelphia, was Article VI added to the Ordinance. When Cutler saw the final

version of the Ordinance, on July 19, he noted in his
diary that the Congress had accepted all but one of his
suggestions. He did not, however, claim Article VI as
one of his suggestions.[19] Poole's assertion that Cutler
was responsible for the slavery prohibition is, then,
subject to the Scotch verdict—not proved.

Poole seems more correct in his conclusion that the
"Ordinance of 1787 and the Ohio purchase were parts of
one and the same transaction. The purchase *would* not
have been made without the Ordinance, and the Ordinance *could* not have been enacted except as an essential condition of the purchase."[20] The Ordinance, in
some form, had been under consideration since at least
1785.[21] It is likely that some Ordinance would have
passed, sooner or later. But the evidence does suggest
that Cutler's lobbying and the interest of the Massachusetts land speculators in purchasing land in Ohio did
spur the Congress to act.

This chronology undermines the third aspect of
Lynd's argument—that Article VI was part of a compromise related to the adoption of the three-fifths clause by
the Constitutional Convention in Philadelphia. Lynd
believed this would explain why a southern majority in
the Congress adopted Article VI. Lynd predicated his
argument on the fact that the final acceptance of the
three-fifths clause took place in Philadelphia on July 12
and that the Ordinance passed in New York on July 13.
Lynd asserted "that a number of men were members of
both Congress and Convention, and communication
between the two bodies was apparently frequent and
full." This led him to conclude that "the essential
features of the Ordinance were reported to members of
the Convention in time to influence its voting on July
12–14," and that "one can justifiably present the hy-
pothesis that there occurred in July 1787 a sectional
compromise involving Congress and Convention, Ordinance and Constitution. . . . " To support this hypoth-
esis, Lynd noted that Manasseh Cutler left New York
after giving his draft of the Ordinance to the Congress,

and that Cutler arrived in Philadelphia on July 12, the same day that the Convention approved the three-fifths clause. Furthermore, Lynd noted that Alexander Hamilton was in New York on July 9 or 10 and in Philadelphia on the 12th. Lynd concluded, "Conceivably, Hamilton left New York late enough to learn the outlines of the Ordinance and arrived in Philadelphia early enough to influence the voting on the twelfth."[22]

There are a number of problems with this analysis. It seems likely that Cutler's amendments to the draft of the Ordinance did not include the three-fifths clause. Nor could Hamilton have known about the clause when he left for Philadelphia, because, as we have already seen, Article VI was added at the very last moment. Finally, it is impossible that the vote in the Convention on the 12th could have been known by the Congress on the 13th, in time to affect the adoption of the Ordinance. And, of course, since the Ordinance was not adopted until the 13th, it seems unlikely that Article VI, which was not introduced until the 13th, could have affected a vote in Philadelphia the day before. It seems more likely that this is simply a coincidence of dates. On the other hand, as I have already indicated, the rest of Lynd's analysis of why a southern majority adopted the Ordinance is sound, persuasive, and insightful.

In the final analysis it may not matter who proposed Article VI, whether Cutler's lobbying made it possible, or why Congress enacted the Ordinance when it did. What is important is that the history of the Ordinance shows: (1) that there was virtually no debate over the slavery provision; (2) that it was added at the last possible moment, without careful consideration; (3) that the rest of the Ordinance was not redrafted to make it consistent with Article VI; and (4) that although the language of Article VI meant that slavery could not exist in the Territory (except for fugitives), it is unlikely that the southern majority which passed the Ordinance understood the Article to mean this.

Whatever the reasons were, the prohibition of slavery

was added to the Ordinance at the eleventh hour. This was not, of course, the first time that a prohibition on slavery in the territories had been considered. In 1784 Jefferson proposed the prohibition of slavery in *all* the national territories after 1800. It is difficult to imagine how Jefferson's proposal would have worked, had it been accepted; by 1800 some of the territories would have probably had large slave populations and politically powerful masters who would have worked to undermine the Ordinance of 1784, had it included Jefferson's prohibition. With no enforcement clause it is impossible to imagine a territorial or state legislature voluntarily ending slavery after the institution had been allowed to grow until 1800. There is no indication that anyone at the time considered or discussed implementation of the proposal. But, the enforcement problems of Jefferson's clause mooted when Congress defeated the proposal with strong and vocal opposition from the southern states.[23]

In 1786 Rufus King of Massachusetts proposed a similar provision, but it too was defeated without debate. Nor was the slavery prohibition debated in 1787. Nathan Dane, King's successor in Congress, also wanted a slavery prohibition, but he initially excluded it from the Ordinance because he thought the attempt would be futile. Why it did pass is unclear. When the last minute amendment was accepted with apparently no discussion, and little comment, Dane could offer no explanation. He wrote King that he had "had no idea the States would agree to the sixth article, prohibiting slavery, as only Massachusetts of the Eastern States, was present," and thus he "omitted it" from the draft; "but finding the House favorably disposed on the subject, after we had completed the other parts, I moved the article, which was agreed to without opposition." No one in the Congress seemed to think this clause was extraordinary. Dane's comments on it in his letter to King were immediately followed by a discussion of what seemed to matter most to Dane, King, and Cutler: the purchase of land in Ohio. Besides Dane, only William Grayson, another member of the committee, commented on the slavery prohibition in any existing letter. The lack of debate on the article or comment on it by members of Congress, especially the many southerners present, suggests that the clause was not considered particularly important.[24]

The lack of debate on the clause and the fact that it was tacked on to the document at the last moment, explains why the rest of the Ordinance conflicts with the famed Article VI. Throughout the Ordinance there are indirect references to slavery.

The main body of the Ordinance guaranteed the property rights of the "French and Canadian inhabitants, and other settlers . . . who have heretofore professed themselves citizens of Virginia." Much of the property owned by these "inhabitants" and "settlers" was slave property. Much litigation in Missouri and Illinois would eventually focus on the status of the slaves owned by these early settlers of the Northwest.[25]

Article II of the Ordinance provided protection for all private property, and required compensation for private property taken for the public good. Did Article VI provide an exception to Article II where slave property was concerned? Article II also provided that the territorial government could never pass legislation which would "interfere with or affect private contracts or engagements, bona fide, and without fraud, previously formed." It would not be farfetched to argue, as many slaveowners would, that slave property purchased or acquired before 1787 could not be taken—or freed—without compensation to the master, and that contracts for the purchase, sale, or rent of slaves, made before 1787, were still enforceable in the Territory. Such an argument would ultimately be made by Chief Justice Taney in *Dred Scott v Sandford*.[26] While Taney's notions of substantive due process may have been inapplicable for the introduction of slavery into a totally unsettled territory, the concept seems somewhat more reasonable for slaves already present in a territory when the federal government extended its jurisdiction over the area.

Another problem for the application of the slavery prohibition in Article VI is that in other places the Ordinance refers to "free male inhabitants" and "free inhabitants." If there were "free inhabitants" then there must also have been "unfree" inhabitants. Slavery and involuntary servitude might have been prohibited in the Northwest Territory, but the congressmen who wrote the Ordinance clearly expected slaves to be there.[27] Indeed, until the eleventh hour addition of Article VI, there was no doubt that slavery would be perfectly legal in the area. But, when Article VI was added the rest of the Ordinance was not rewritten; thus, the Ordinance contained logical and linguistic contradictions. These would enable slaveowners in the Northwest to argue that their property rights had not been affected by Article VI.

Finally, Article IV of the Ordinance provided for free navigation of the "waters leading into the Mississippi and St. Lawrence, and the carrying places between the same" for all Americans. It is doubtful that the congressmen from the southern states, as well as the representatives from such slave states as New York and New Jersey, who voted for the Ordinance, understood it to mean that they could not take their slaves with them when traveling on the nation's important inland water routes.[28]

Despite the intentions of Dane and others to guarantee that the Northwest would be "free soil," Article VI of the Ordinance was ill-suited to the task. It contained no enforcement clause, such as the Civil War Amendments to the United States Constitution would have. The Article did not indicate what organ of government—the territorial governor, the territorial judiciary, the territorial legislature (which would not be formed until the territory's population reached "five thousand free male inhabitants of full age"), or the national Congress—would take action to end slavery.

Since an end to slavery would require an innovative change in public policy and social institutions, some governmental intervention was necessary. In its failure to provide a mechanism for enforcement, Article VI must be compared and contrasted to other parts of the Ordinance. Article III, for example, declared that "schools and the means of education shall forever be encouraged." But it neither required that schools be built nor did it provide an enforcement mechanism. In this way Article III and Article VI are similar. But the substance of the Articles was so different that in one an enforcement mechanism was unnecessary while in the other it was vital.

A requirement that schools be built, or a declaration of what governmental body should do so, was unnecessary because for more than a century public schools had been built by local communities in America. Americans knew what schools were and knew how to build them, but few Americans had any experience with dismantling an entrenched social system that provided wealth for those who had political power at the expense of those who lacked all power. The education clause could be implemented by those who would benefit from the clause, but those people who would most directly benefit from Article VI were prohibited from participating in the political process, and thus could not insure the implementation of the Article. Finally, both the creation of public schools and the abolition of slavery would have financial costs. While the Ordinance of 1787 provided no funds for either object, the Land Ordinance of 1785 had provided that one lot in each township would be reserved "for the maintenance of public schools within the said township."[29] Thus, the national government had committed financial resources to the education provisions of Article III but not the prohibition of slavery requiried by Article VI.

Article III also dealt with Indians, admonishing the settlers to treat them fairly and not take their property without their consent. Unlike slaves, the Indians were in a position to defend their property rights, either in court or on the battlefield. As Peter Onuf has argued, "emigration to the Northwest" was "sluggish . . . because it took so long to pacify the Indian frontier." The settlers knew that peaceful relations with the Indians might be maintained if this provision of Article III were carried out; thus, this part of Article III could be enforced. Just to make sure, however, Article III also reserved for Congress the right to declare war and explicitly directed that "laws founded in justice and humanity" would "be made" to protect Indian rights. The Indian policy was clear: either the settlers would observe "good faith" toward the Indians or the Congress would intervene.[30] No such threat of intervention existed for Article VI, nor were the settlers in the territory even admonished to treat the slavery prohibition with "good faith."

The slavery prohibition compared unfavorably to both the education and the Indian provisions of Article III. Those who would benefit most from Article VI lacked the political power to implement it, the legal rights or support to enforce it in court, or the military might to fight for it on the battlefield. Neither the Congress nor the Territorial government were directed to pass any enforcement legislation. Moreover, those in the Territory who had the power to implement the slavery prohibition were the men least likely to do so.

Besides failing to indicate how the slavery prohibition was to be enforced, the framers of the Ordinance did not resolve the internal contradictions created by Article VI. The meaning of Article VI was left to whoever held power in the Territory. If nothing else, the Ordinance is worth reading and studying as an example of *how not to* draft a statute. It serves to remind legislators, lawyers, and jurists that hastily drafted and poorly planned amendments to legislation, added at the last minute, may not accomplish what their authors wish. Had there been a full fledged debate over Article VI a clearer sense of its meaning might have emerged. In such a debate someone might have asked if the Ordinance was meant to free the slaves then living in the Territory. Similarly, a debate over Article VI might have clarified the status of the children of slaves in the region. Something modeled along Pennsylvania's gradual emancipation statute might have emerged, which would have specified the status of the existing slaves, their children, and any slaves brought into the Territory, either as transients, sojourners, or residents. However, the Ordinance was passed when there were no delegates present from Pennsylvania, Rhode Island, or Connecticut, where gradual emancipation statutes already existed.[31] In fact, all of the delegates who voted for the Ordinance came from states where emancipation had never been a political issue[32]; thus, the exact meaning of Article VI, and how it was to be implemented, was not debated and remained in doubt.

In another context, the Ordinance can be seen as an example of the tension between liberty and property inherent in Revolutionary America. Over the years, "The Ordinance has become a symbol of the Revolution's liberalism" toward race, at least in part, because it was the only important act by the national government under the Articles of Confederation which indicated disapproval for the peculiar institution. But even this symbol is an uncertain one. Just as the "self evident" truths of the Declaration of Independence—"that all men are created equal," and endowed with the rights to "Life, Liberty and the pursuit of Happiness"—were proclaimed by a man who owned nearly two hundred slaves, so too, the Ordinance declared an end to slavery while at the same time protecting the property rights of slaveowners living in the Northwest. Late eighteenth century Americans were trapped in an ideology of private property that made it almost impossible for them to collectively give up their own pursuit of happiness for the liberty of others.[33] In the Ordinance, the ideals of liberty came into conflict with the selfish happiness of the ruling race; thus, Congress could easily declare there would be no slavery in the Northwest Territory. It was quite another matter to eliminate the institution there.

III. Slavery and the Old Northwest

Whatever it was supposed to accomplish, the Ordinance had little immediate impact on the legal status of slaves in the Territory. Most of the Territory's slaves lived in what would eventually become Indiana and Illinois.[34] This area had been French until 1763, when Britain took possession through the Peace of Paris. This treaty guaranteed the property rights of the original French settlers. In 1779 George Rogers Clark seized the Northwest and claimed it for his home state under Virginia's 1609 charter. Although never intending to govern the area indefinitely, for a variety of political reasons Virginia continued to assert authority over the Territory until 1784. Virginia's act of cession transferring possession of the area to the national government also protected the property rights of the residents of the Territory. Thus, when the Territory came into the hands of the United States, slaveowners were living there and the national government was obligated to protect their property.[35]

Shortly after the adoption of the Ordinance, settlers in what later became Indiana and Illinois appointed Barthelemi Tardiveau to lobby Congress on matters of concern to the Northwest. Although the Ordinance contained no enforcement provision, and would in fact remain unenforced for many years, it nevertheless troubled the Territory's slaveowners. The Franco-American slaveowners, coming out of a civil law tradition, may have believed that the Ordinance was self-enforcing, or would be enforced by the national government. In July 1788 Tardiveau petitioned Congress "By order & in behalf of the french [sic.] inhabitants of the Illinois [country]." The petitioners asked for security for certain land titles, reimbursement for goods impressed by American soldiers, and protection of the rights of the French settlers. The petition concluded by noting:

> There is in an Ordinance of Congress, an Ex post facto law
> . . . which declares that Slavery Shall not take place in the
> Western territory. Many of the inhabitants of these districts
> have Slaves, and Some have no other property but Slaves. If
> they wish to preserve their property they must transport
> themselves to the Spanish Side of the Mississippi; but if they
> do, they Shall lose the lands granted them by Congress. One
> law tells them: leave the country, or ye Shall forfeit your
> negroes; the other Saith; Stay in the country, or your lands
> shall be taken from ye. [36]

The French settlers hoped Congress would resolve their dilemma by allowing them to keep their slaves in the Territory and thus hold on to their lands as well. When this request received no action Tardiveau presented a second petition which requested Congress either to modify the slavery prohibition of the Ordinance or to "abrogate that part of their Resolve which binds them to a three years residence in the country in order to be entitled to the property of lands granted them." Once again Tardiveau asserted that the slavery prohibition of the Ordinance "operates as an Ex post facto law."[37]

The Illinois Country settlers believed that the Ordinance violated their property rights. Article VI could not technically be considered an ex post facto law,[38] but the assertion that it was such a law underscored the popular hostility to it. Ex post facto laws symbolized tyranny and oppression; they were also simply bad policy. It was against such arbitrary lawmaking that the Revolution was fought. The new national Constitution would prohibit them in the United States. The message from Tardiveau and the other French settlers was clear: by destroying property rights in slaves the Congress was violating its revolutionary commitment to fair

government and the protection of private property.
Justice and human liberty were not an issue for the
slaveowners of the Northwest.

For many of those living in the Illinois Country the
new United States was simply another "government."
Since 1763 the area had been ruled by France, Great
Britain, and Virginia. Certainly the settlers could not
have felt great attachments for the United States. The
Revolution had not been *their* revolution. Thus, when
the Congress failed to respond positively to their petitions many of the French settlers voted with their feet.
In July 1789 Major John Hamtramck reported that "The
King [of Spain] has permitted the inhabitants living on
the American side to settle themselves" in the Spanish
territory west of the Mississippi. A few weeks later he
noted that "A number of people had gone & were about
to go from the Illinois side to the Spanish Side, in
consequence of a resolve of Congress respecting negroes
who. . .were to be free."[39]

Tardiveau did not blame the slaveowners for leaving.
He explained to Territorial Governor Arthur St. Clair
that "The wretched inhabitants of Illinois, who had
seen themselves neglected for ten years by that [na-
tional] power from which alone they could expect protection, now found that the very first act of attention
paid to them pronounced their ruin." The Ordinance
had sparked "many aggravating" rumors "that the very
moment" the territorial Governor arrived "all their
slaves would be set free." Upon hearing those rumors, a
"panic seized upon their minds" and the wealthiest
settlers sought "from the Spanish Government that
security which they conceived was refused to them" by
the United States."[40]

Those slaveowners who remained in the Northwest
quickly discovered that the words of the Ordinance were
much like the words of the Declaration of Independence. They sounded idealistic, but had little force. Although Congress refused to modify the Ordinance along
the lines suggested by Tardiveau's petitions, neither did

Congress take any steps to implement the Ordinance. Tardiveau explained to St. Clair that he had not pressured Congress for a definitive answer to his memorial because "it was needless" and he had already "troubled that body with a number of petitions." Tardiveau assured St. Clair that "gentlemen [in Congress] remarked that the intention of the obnoxious resolution had been solely to prevent the future importation of slaves into the Federal country; that it was not meant to affect the rights of the ancient inhabitants." Tardiveau wanted St. Clair to convey this information to the settlers in the Territory. In the summer of 1789 Tardiveau wrote friends in Illinois that "the resolve of Congress respecting the Slavery of this Country was not intended to extend to the negroes of the old French inhabitants." Major Hamtramck "immediately published" this information in an effort to stem the tide of emigration from the Northwest.[41]

Tardiveau was not entirely correct in his assessment of Congressional intent. The Congress had in fact made no dispositive interpretation of Article VI of the Ordinance. Rather, Tardiveau's petitions had been referred to a committee made up of Abraham Clark of New Jersey, Hugh Williamson of North Carolina, and James Madison of Virginia. This committee offered a resolution to the Congress which declared that the:

> Ordinance for the government of the Western territory, shall not be construed to deprive the Inhabitants of Kaskaskies Illinois, Post St. Vincents, and the Other Villages formerly settled by the French and Canadians, of their Rights and property in Negro and other Slaves, which they were possessed of at the time of the said Ordinance, or in any manner to Manumit or Set free any such negroes or other persons under Servitude within any part of s^{d}. Western territory; any thing in the said Ordinance to the contrary notwithstanding.[42]

This proposed resolution was never brought before the Congress for debate or a vote. Therefore, it could not really be said to explain Congressional intent. At

best it indicated what some men in Congress believed to
be the best application of the Ordinance. As the new
Constitution of the United States went into effect, the
meaning of the Ordinance, passed under the old Articles of Confederation, remained unclear.

On another level, however, this committee report is a
significant indication of sentiment on the issue. The
report suggests how truly *uncommitted* the Founders
were to ending slavery. James Madison's presence on this
committee is particularly important. On the eve of the
adoption of the Constitution the "father" of that document failed to interpret the Ordinance in an antislavery
light, despite the language of the Ordinance, which
would have supported such an interpretation. If a man
with Madison's values, stature, and intellectual accom-
plishments could not take a stronger position on liberat-
ing the slaves in the Northwest, then it is perhaps not
surprising that others of the Founding generation failed
to confront the problems of slavery where the institution was more entrenched and the number of slaves was
greater.

The committee report seemed to distort the plain
meaning of the Ordinance. The committee urged the
Congress to "construe" the Ordinance to mean that
slaves living in the Territory were not in fact emanci-
pated, and that the French inhabitants (and by this time
a good many Anglo-American inhabitants as well)
would not be deprived of their property under the Ordinance. Slaveowners throughout the nation assumed
that their property right in slaves included a right to the
children of their female slaves. The committee report
therefore implied some sort of perpetual slavery for the
descendants of those slaves living in the Territory in
1787. The committee asked Congress to accept this
construction "any thing in the said Ordinance to the
contrary notwithstanding." Such a statement implies
that the committee felt the language of the Ordinance
was "to the contrary" and that the proffered construction violated the plain meaning of the clause.

Like the Congressional committee, Governor St. Clair had no interest in interfering in the master-slave relations of those he governed. Despite the language of the Ordinance, the Governor saw no reason to take action to end slavery. In 1790 he reported to President Washington that settlers were still emigrating to New Spain to protect their slave property. To help stop this de-population St. Clair told the President:

> I have thought it proper to explain the Article respecting Slaves as a prohibition to any future introduction of them, but not to extend to the liberation of those the People were already possessed of, and acquired under the Sanction of the Laws they were subject, at the same time I have given them to understand that Steps would probably be taken for the gradual abolition of Slavery, with which they seem perfectly satisfied.[43]

This interpretation assumed that the Ordinance was only a directive to the Territorial authorities, and that without further legislation slavery might continue. St. Clair was, however, concerned about satisfying the desires of his white, slaveholding constituency, and not with any rights slaves might have under the Ordinance. No one in the new national government challenged St. Clair's interpretation, perhaps because Washington and his cabinet agreed with it.

However, a year later, St. Clair revealed to Secretary of State Thomas Jefferson that neither he nor his constituents were happy with his earlier interpretation of the Ordinance. His initial understanding of the Ordinance would prevent the return of those slaveholders who had emigrated to the Spanish territory because they thought the Ordinance would free their slaves. St. Clair felt that those slaveowners who had left the Territory should be allowed to return with their slaves. The governor was certain "that the [Spanish] Country itself is much less desirable than on the American side— could they be allowed to bring them [their slaves] with them, all those who retired from that Cause would return to a man."[44]

Two years later the Territorial Governor no longer wished to be held to either of the interpretations he offered Washington and Jefferson. St. Clair wrote that the Ordinance was "no more than the Declaration of a Principle which was to Govern the Legislature in all Acts respecting that matter, and the Courts of Justice in their Decisions upon Cases arising after the Date of the Ordinance." This idea had been implied in his 1790 letter to Washington. Now he spelled it out. St. Clair went further still in reinterpreting the Ordinance. He asserted that

> the Sense of Congress is very well to be known on this Subject by what they have actually done—Viz: By making it unlawful to import into any of the States any Negroes after a certain specified Time, and which is yet to come—so that if any person after the Arrival of that period should import a Cargoe of Negroes there is no Doubt that they would all be free while those that were in the Country before remain in Slavery according to the former laws.[45]

St. Clair never had an opportunity to implement this interpretation of the Ordinance, but, he did use his office to discourage pro-freedom interpretations of the Ordinance. In 1794 Territorial Judge George Turner issued a writ of habeas corpus for slaves owned by another territorial official, Henry Vanderburgh. Turner asserted that all slaves were "free by the Constitution of the Territory" but before the case could come to trial a group of men, allegedly employed by Vanderburgh, kidnapped the blacks and reenslaved them. Turner sought indictments for kidnapping against Vanderburgh and his associates, but St. Clair interceded to protect the kidnappers. St. Clair also informed Turner that the Ordinance was prospective only, and could not be used to emancipate slaves living in the Territory before 1787.[46]

Turner subsequently attempted to emancipate other slaves through the use of habeas corpus. Slaveowners complained to St. Clair about Turner, and residents of the Illinois Country petitioned Congress to remove him from office. This pressure was successful. In 1796 United States Attorney General Charles Lee reported to the House of Representatives that Turner should be prosecuted in a territorial court for abusing his office, and if convicted, he might then be impeached and removed from office. In 1797 a Congressional committee concurred with Lee's advice, and under these threats Judge Turner resigned his office and left the Territory.[47]

At the end of Washington's administration the status of slaves in the Northwest remained substantially what it had been before the Ordinance. The Territorial governor had publicly and privately asserted that the Ordinance applied only to those slaves brought into the Northwest *after* 1787. Slaveholders in the Territory, who were often the most politically powerful men in the region, were not, however, content with this interpretation. Some had brought slaves into the Territory since the adoption of the Ordinance. Others hoped to bring more slaves into the Territory. As of 1797 no slaves appear to have been freed by the Ordinance; however, the language of the Ordinance posed a potential threat to slavery north of the Ohio River, especially for those who owned slaves brought to the Territory after July 1787. In the early years of the nineteenth century slaveowners would petition Congress to modify the Ordinance, to protect their slaves. These petitions, like earlier ones, would produce sympathetic committee reports, but no new legislation.[48] In the meantime, the Territorial governments in Indiana and Illinois would adopt laws to protect slavery and involuntary servitude in those territories.[49]

IV. An Ambiguous Legacy

The inconsistencies between the promise of the Ordinance and its reality were ignored by most nineteenth century northerners, who in fact tended to venerate the Northwest Ordinance, in part because of Article VI.

Much of this veneration was politically motivated. Those who opposed slavery sought to wrap themselves in the memory of the Founders. Article VI enabled them to do this. Antislavery activists like Edward Coles and Salmon P. Chase persistently argued that the framers of the Ordinance intended to make the Northwest forever free. When, therefore, an attempt was made to make Illinois a slave state, the words of the Ordinance and the memory of those who were involved in its passage were an important weapon for Edward Coles and his antislavery supporters. Similarly, in his arguments before various courts, Chase asserted that the Ordinance meant that slaves became free the moment they arrived in Ohio, unless they had escaped from one of the original states, as provided by the fugitive slave provision of Article VI. While no court ever accepted this second argument, Chase was successful in making antislavery appear to be a legitimate part of the American Constitutional tradition that began with the Ordinance. The black community of Cincinnati praised Chase for being a "firm, zealous and devoted friend" to those "friendless objects of slaveholding cupidity" who "have found themselves by the providence of God, upon our soil, and have sought through the instrumentality of the Ordinance of 1787, enacted by the wisdom and patriotism of the Founders of the American Revolution, to assert their claims to those rights which our boasted Declaration of Independence declares to be inalienable."[50]

Even politicians not noted for their abolitionist sentiments praised the Ordinance. For example, during the Webster-Hayne debate, Daniel Webster not only used the Ordinance to his advantage, but tried to claim that a Massachusetts man, Nathan Dane, deserved the credit for its passage. Thomas Hart Benton, who also opposed South Carolina's extremism, invoked the Ordinance as well, but claimed the glory of ending slavery in the region for a Southerner, Thomas Jefferson.[51]

The use of the Ordinance in the debates over slavery

suggests its impact on the nation's political culture, but its impact on slavery in the Northwest, especially in what became Indiana and Illinois, is more ambiguous. Slavery continued in Indiana until after statehood. Not until 1820, in *State* v. *Lasselle*, did the Indiana Supreme Court declare that the institution violated the new state constitution. Even then, a few slaves were held until the 1830s.[52]

In Illinois the record is even bleaker. Here slavery continued to be vigorous throughout the territorial period. Illinois probably would have adopted a full-fledged system of slavery in 1818 if the territorial leaders had not been certain that Congress would not have granted statehood under such a constitution.[53] Fear of a rejection of such a constitution by Congress, and not the dictates of the Ordinance, preserved Illinois as a nominally free state. Nevertheless, slaveholders in Illinois were powerful enough to protect the institution in the state's constitution of 1818 and in subsequent legislation.[54] No slaves living in the state were explicitly freed under the constitution and, unlike its Indiana counterpart, the Illinois Supreme Court did not interpret either the Ordinance or its own state Constitution to have ended slavery. On the contrary, the state supreme court continued to support slavery and servitude in the state until the 1840s. Not until Illinois adopted a second Constitution in 1848 did the Prairie State finally abolish slavery.[55]

The legacy of the Ordinance is, then, a mixed one. The Ordinance certainly helped put slavery on the road to ultimate extinction in the Northwest, but that road proved to be an extraordinarily long one. In the early 1820s Illinois came within a few hundred votes of reversing its direction. At that point, immigration from the Northeast and the lure of cotton for slaveholders probably had more to do with preventing a change in the Constitution than did the dictates of the Northwest Ordinance.[56]

A more clearly drafted Ordinance might have provided

a better guide to the legislators of the Northwest. Such clarification might have prevented the struggle to completely legalize slavery in Illinois in 1823–24. It might also have led to freedom for the two to three thousand blacks who remained enslaved in Indiana and Illinois between 1787 and 1848.[57] In at least one small corner of revolutionary America the legacy of freedom written into Article VI would then have been a reality to those who were denied their natural rights under existing laws. Instead, the legacy remained ambiguous and unfulfilled for over six decades.

---

1. Portions of this article appeared in "Slavery and the Northwest Ordinance: A Study in Ambiguity," *Journal of the Early Republic* 6 (Winter 1986): 343–70. The author acknowledges the permission of that journal to reprint parts of that article here.

2. Salmon P. Chase, ed., *The Statutes of Ohio and the Northwestern Territory* (Cincinnati, 1833), 1:17-18; Edward Coles, *History of the Ordinance of 1787* (Philadelphia, 1856), 32-33; Abraham Lincoln, Speech at Cincinnati, Ohio, September 1859, in Roy P. Basler, ed., *The Collected Works of Abraham Lincoln*, 9 vols. (New Brunswick, N.J., 1953–55), 3:454–57.

3. The Southwest Ordinance was not written until after the Northwest Ordinance was passed. However, slavery was well entrenched in the Southwest by 1787. The fact that Jefferson's attempt to prohibit slavery in all the western territories after 1800 was defeated in 1784 further supports the notion that everyone in Congress understood that the Southwest would be open to slavery if the institution was prohibited in the Northwest. A similar analysis was made in "The Compromise of 1787," reprinted in Staughton Lynd, ed., *Class Conflict, Slavery and the United States Constitution* (Indianapolis, 1967), 185–213. Article VI may also have strengthened slavery in the South by preventing competition between the Ohio Valley and Virginia and Kentucky.

4. The fugitive slave clause of the Ordinance was the first important protection given to slavery by the national government. The Constitutional Convention did not consider a fugitive slave provision until August 28, a month and a half after the Ordinance provided such protection for slaveowners. It is likely that the South Carolinians at the Convention who demanded this clause got the idea for such a clause from the Ordinance. Max Farrand, ed., *The Records of the Federal Convention of 1787*, 4 vols. (New Haven, 1937), 2:443, 453–54. The vigorous defense of slavery by the deep south delegates to the Convention stands in contrast to the adoption of Article VI of the Ordinance, if that article is seen as "antislavery."

However, it is likely that the Deep South delegates in Congress thought the Article would protect slavery where it was and allow it to spread to the Southwest; thus, they may have seen the article as proslavery, or at least as protective of slavery.

5. Peter S. Onuf, "From Constitution to Higher Law: The Reinterpretation of the Northwest Ordinance," *Ohio History* 94 (Winter-Spring 1985): 5–33.

6. Cases throughout the antebellum period raised the problem that persons might be held as slaves in an area where slavery itself was prohibited. See generally Paul Finkelman, *An Imperfect Union* (Chapel Hill, 1981). The problem of enslavement without the sanction of law persists to this day. In *United States* v. *Mussry*, 726 F2d. 1448 (1984), a federal court in California ruled that the coercion necessary to produce slavery need not be physical, but could be a result of threats, especially if those enslaved were aliens unfamiliar with the laws of the United States. In *Mussry* the court allowed the prosecution of persons who had enticed Indonesian aliens to the United States, then seized their passports and return airline tickets, and told the Indonesians that they would suffer terrible penalties if they tried to escape. Such a case illustrates the power of a "master" over illiterate minorities, be they Indonesians in late twentieth century California or "indentured servants" in early nineteenth century Indiana and Illinois.

7. *Marchand v. Negro Peggy*, 2 S. & R. 118 (1815). Holding Peggy to be a slave, Tilghman declared: "The only just mode of extirpating the small remains of slavery in the state, would be by purchasing the slaves at a reasonable price, and paying their owners out of the public treasury." *Id.* at 19. *Jarrot (colored man)* v. *Jarrot*, 2 Gil. (Ill.) 1 (1845).

8. On the problems of slavery and the conflict-of-laws, see Finkelman, *An Imperfect Union. Somerset* v. *Stewart*, Loft 1 (1772); 20 Howell St. Tr. 1 (1772). See also William M. Wiecek, *The Sources of Antislavery Constitutionalism in America, 1760–1848* (Ithaca, 1977), 20–39. For discussions of slavery in the North see arguments of counsel in *Commonwealth v. Aves*, 18 Pick. (Mass.) 193 (1836); *Lemmon v. The People*, 20 N.Y. 562 (1860).

9. Northwest Ordinance, Sec. 14.

10. *Journals of the Continental Congress, 1774-1789* (Washington, 1936), 32:283, 313–20, 333. The only dissenting vote in the entire Congress was Abraham Yates of New York.

11. Nineteenth century historians sought to determine who deserved the credit for the Ordinance in general and Article VI in particular. Much of this writing was clearly filiopietistic. In attempting to duck the issue George Bancroft wrote: "Thomas Jefferson first summoned Congress to prohibit slavery in all the territory of the United States; Rufus King lifted up the measure when it lay almost lifeless on the ground. . .a congress . . . headed by William Grayson, supported by Richard Henry Lee, and using Nathan Dane as scribe, carried the measure to the goal. . . . " *History of the United States of America, From the Discovery of the Continent*, 6 vols. (New York, 1883–1885), 6:290. At the time the Ordinance was passed only one state present, Massachusetts, had ended slavery. Five others, Delaware, Virginia, South Carolina, North Carolina, and Georgia, would retain slavery until the Civil War. The two remaining states, New York and New Jersey, would not adopt gradual emancipation statutes until 1799 and 1804.

12. Lynd, "The Compromise of 1787," 199. Lynd also argues that the South was anxious to pass the Ordinance so that the American side of the Mississippi River would be quickly settled. Such a settlement would strengthen America's hand in negotiating with the Spanish for access to New Orleans. This explains why southerners were anxious to have some bill for organizing the territory, but does not explain why southerners should have been willing to give up slavery in the area.

13. Peter Onuf, The Origins of the Federal Republic: Jurisdictional Controversies in the United States, 1775–1787 (Philadelphia, 1983), 169–71.

14. Ibid. William Grayson to James Monroe, New York, August 8, 1787, in Edmund C. Burnett, ed., Letters of Members of the Continental Congress, 8 vols. (Washington, 1921–1936), 8:631–33. Grayson's argument suggests that Deep South congressmen may have supported Article VI because prohibiting slavery in the Northwest would lower the price of slaves in the Southeast and Southwest while Upper South congressmen supported the Ordinance to avoid economic competition from north of the Ohio River. Peter Force, "The Ordinance of 1787 and Its History," in William Henry Smith, The St. Clair Papers: The Life and Public Services of Arthur St. Clair, 2 vols. (Cincinnati, 1882), 2:611–12.

15. Richard Henry Lee to Francis Lightfoot Lee, July 14, 1787, in Burnett, ed., Letters of Members, 8:619-20; Richard Henry Lee to George Washington, ibid., 620.

16. William Frederick Poole, The Ordinance of 1787, and Dr. Manasseh Cutler as an Agent in its Formation (Cambridge, 1876), 26, 27.

17. Ibid., 29; Journal of Congress, 32:343. Jack Eblen, The First and Second United States Empires: Governors and Territorial Government, 1784–1912 (Pittsburgh, 1968), 43n, denies that Cutler could have had any effect on the Ordinance because "it is clear that by the time Cutler arrived in New York in 1787, there was nothing really new to be offered." However, Article VI, containing the slavery prohibition and the quite new fugitive slave provision, was in fact added to the Ordinance after Cutler left New York. Eblen is confused about when Cutler appeared in New York. Eblen claims Cutler arrived in New York on May 9 (page 37), and predicates his analysis accordingly. However, Cutler did not in fact come to New York until July 6.

18. Jay A. Barrett, Evolution of the Ordinance of 1787 (New York, 1891, Anro Press reprint, 1971), 74-77, argues against Cutler's antislavery credentials.

19. William Parker Cutler and Julia Perkins Cutler, Life, Journals, and Correspondence of Rev. Manasseh Cutler, LL.D., 2 vols. (Cincinnati, 1888), 1:343–44, 230, 242, 293. See also, Edmund C. Burnett, The Continental Congress (New York, 1941), 685. The reliability of the printed journals of Cutler has also been questioned, although not on this point. Lee Nathaniel Newcomer, "Manasseh Cutler's Writings: A Note on Editorial Practice," Mississippi Valley Historical Review, 47 (June 1960): 88–101.

20. Poole, The Ordinance of 1787, 31.

21. Robert F. Berkhofer, Jr., "Jefferson, The Ordinance of 1784 and the Origins of the American Territorial System," William and Mary Quarterly 29 (April 1972): 231–62. See also Onuf, The Origins of the Federal Republic, Chap. 7.

22. Lynd, "Compromise of 1787," 187, 207, 210, 211.

23. Berkhofer, "Jefferson, The Ordinance of 1784," discusses the defeat

of Jefferson's prohibition on slavery. According to Merrill D. Peterson, the Ordinance of 1784 ultimately proved to be "ineffectual." *Thomas Jefferson and the New Nation* (New York, 1970), 283. Even if Jefferson's proposal had been accepted, it might never have been implemented. Most Jeffersonian scholars refuse to consider that Jefferson's proposal was also unworkable because of its potential enforcement problems. By proposing that slavery be allowed to flourish until 1800 Jefferson was following his life-long policy of denouncing slavery but postponing any action until later. One exception to this scholarship is William Cohen's important article, "Thomas Jefferson and the Problem of Slavery," *Journal of American History* 56 (December 1969). Cohen notes, at 511, that under Jefferson's proposal "bondage would have been legal in the area for sixteen years; and it seems likely that, if the institution of slavery had been allowed to get a foothold in the territory, the prohibition would have been repealed."

24. Nathan Dane to Rufus King, New York, July 16, 1787, in Burnett, *Letters of Members* 8:621–22. The editors of the forthcoming edition of the letters of members of the Continental Congress at the Library of Congress have been kind enough to share their materials for this period. Except for the letters cited above there appear to be no existing letters indicating that anyone at the Congress even mentioned the slavery prohibition to anyone. Of the sixteen letters written to or from southern congressmen in the month following the passage of the Ordinance, only the Grayson letter cited in note 14 mentioned the slavery provision. Burnett, *Letters of Members* 8:619–639.

25. Northwest Ordinance, Sec. 2. For example, in Missouri see *Merry v. Tiffin and Menard*, 1 Mo. 725 (1827); *Theoteste v. Chouteau*, 2 Mo. 144 (1829); and *Nancy v. Trammel*, 3 Mo. 306 (1836); *Chouteau and Keizer v. Hope*, 7 Mo. 428 (1842); *Chouteau v. Pierre (of Color)*, 9 Mo. 3 (1845); *Charlotte (of Color) v. Chouteau*, 11 Mo. 193 (1847); reargued at 21 Mo. 590 (1855); 25 Mo. 465 (1857); 33 Mo. 194 (1862). In Illinois the leading case is *Jarrot v. Jarrot*, 2 Gilman 1 (1845). A number of other Illinois cases involved slaves brought into the Illinois territory after 1787 by the French settlers. *Boon v. Juliet*, 1 Scammon 258 (1836); *Choisser v. Hargrave*, 1 Scammon 317 (1836); *Borders v. Borders*, 4 Scammon 341 (1843). Apparently a number of cases involving the "French" slaves went unreported. Roger D. Bridges, ed., "John Mason Peck on Illinois Slavery," *Journal of the Illinois State Historical Society* 75 (Autumn 1982): 201. Slaves brought to Illinois before 1787 were referred to as "French" slaves even if they were owned by Anglo-Americans.

26. *Dred Scott v. Sandford*, 19 Howard (U.S.) 393 (1857). See generally, Don Fehrenbacher, *The Dred Scott Case* (New York, 1978).

27. Northwest Ordinance, Sec. 9 and Art. V. It is unlikely that the Congressmen were making a distinction between indentured servants and others when they used the term "free inhabitants." For one thing, indentured servants, like apprentices, were usually considered "free," even though they might be under some sort of long-term contract. This is clearly the understanding of the Constitution's 3/5th clause, Art. I, Sec. 2, Par. 3. The Articles of Confederation are less clear on this issue. Article IV talks about "the free inhabitants of each of these states" and excludes "paupers, vagabonds, and fugitives from justice." It seems likely that this clause included indentured persons as "free inhabitants." Article IX of the Articles of Confederation allocates quotas for military enlistments based

on "the number of white inhabitants." This certainly included indentured servants. In a strictly legal sense indentured servants were free persons who *voluntarily* contracted to serve someone for a term of years. As such they were not in "involuntary servitude."

28. Northwest Ordinance, Art. IV. See *State v. Hoppess*, 2 Western L. J. 279 (1845) where Judge Nathaniel Read of the Ohio Supreme Court refused to free a slave whose master voluntarily allowed him to leave a boat which was temporarily docked in Cincinnati. Read believed that the Ohio River wharves were open to unrestricted transit for all Americans, including masters traveling with their slaves. See generally, Finkelman, *An Imperfect Union*. New York did not take steps to end slavery until 1799. "An Act for the gradual abolition of slavery," passed March 19, 1799, *New York Laws*, 1799, Chap. 62. New Jersey did not act until 1804, "An Act for the gradual abolition of slavery," *New Jersey Session Laws 1804*, 251. At the time there was no indication that New York or New Jersey would end slavery in the near future. See Arthur Zilversmit, *The First Emancipation* (Chicago, 1967). James Madison told the Virginia ratifying convention in 1788 that these two states "would probably oppose any attempts to annihilate this species of property" because they "had made no attempt, or taken any step, to take them away from the people." Jonathan Elliot, ed., *Debates in the Several State Conventions on the Adoption of the Federal Constitution*, 2d ed., 5 vols. (Philadelphia, 1888), 3:459.

29. "An Ordinance for ascertaining the mode of disposing of Lands in the Western Territory," Act of May 20, 1785, *Journals of the Continental Congress*, 38:375–81, quotation at 378.

30. Onuf, "From Constitution to Higher Law," 19. Article II of the Ordinance guaranteed basic civil liberties, such as access to the writ of habeas corpus, jury trial, a right to bail, and prohibition of cruel and unusual punishments. These protections could be enforced by the people of the territory through their elected representatives, through petitions to Congress, or through appeals to courts. With the exception of initiating litigation, slaves in the Northwest had no way to vindicate their rights. Initiating legal action was difficult for slaves, who could not testify against whites, and who had little or no money, a lack of mobility, and low levels of literacy. Furthermore, litigation subjected slaves to retaliation from their masters. A comparison of Articles II and VI suggests that granting constitutional rights to people is only effective if those people have the power and resources to protect their rights.

31. "An Act for the Gradual Abolition of Slavery," *Pennsylvania Acts, 1780*. "An Act authorizing the manumission of negroes, mulattoes, and others, and for the gradual abolition of slavery," *Rhode Island Laws, 1784*; "An Act concerning Indian, mulatto, and negro servants and slaves," *Connecticut Laws, 1784*.

32. Massachusetts had abolished slavery through its Constitution and judicial decision. Emancipation had been a political issue in Massachusetts only to the the the extent that the 1778 Massachusetts Constitution did not have a free and equal clause and because it discriminated against blacks. Willi Paul Adams, *The First American Constitutions: Republican Ideology and the Making of State Constitutions in the Revolutionary Era* (Chapel Hill, 1980), 184. However, to be charitable to Dane and others, when dealing with great social issues—with such monumental questions as human freedom—it may be better to pass what legislation you can, when

you can, than to wait in hopes that something better can be accomplished at a later date.

33. This problem is also considered in Donald Robinson, *Slavery in the Structure of American Politics, 1765–1820* (New York, 1971). Linda Grant De Pauw has demonstrated that very few Americans in the Revolutionary period had the liberty to pursue happiness. Women, minors, propertyless white adults males, free blacks, and, of course, slaves faced numerous legal restrictions that limited their opportunities and rights. Linda Grant De Pauw, "Land of the Unfree: Legal Limitations on Liberty in Pre-Revolutionary America," *Maryland History Magazine*, 68 (Winter 1973): 355.

34. While population figures for this period are unreliable, all evidence indicates that all but a handful of the slaves in the Northwest lived in what later became Indiana and Illinois. N. Dwight Harris, *The History of Negro Servitude in Illinois* (Chicago, 1904); Emma Lou Thornbrough, *The Negro in Indiana* (Indianapolis, 1957). All of the petitions to Congress in favor of allowing slavery in the Northwest came from the area that would become Indiana and Illinois. There were no doubt a few, but very few, slaves in what would become the states of Ohio and Michigan.

35. Onuf, *Origins of the Federal Republic*, 75–77. William M. Malloy, et al., eds., *Treaties, Conventions, International Acts, Protocols, and Agreements Between the United States and Other Powers, 1776–1937*, 4 vols. (1910–1938), 1:586; "An act to authorize the delegates of this state in congress, to convey to the United States, in congress assembled, all the rights of this commonwealth to the territory north westward of the river Ohio," Act of October 1783, 11 Hening 326.

36. "Memorial of Barthelemi Tardiveau, July 8, 1788," in Clarence W. Alvord, ed., *Kaskaskia Records, 1778–1790* (Springfield, 1909), 475–88. See also, Arthur C. Boggess, *The Settlement of Illinois, 1778–1830* (Freeport, N.Y., 1970, reprint of 1908 edition), 50–53.

37. "Memorial of Berthelemi Tardiveau, September 17, 1788," in *Kaskaskia Records*, 491–93.

38. An *ex post facto* law makes conduct criminal (or changes the penalty or punishment for such conduct, or the rules of evidence to prove such conduct) subsequent to the conduct. Since the holding of slaves was not made criminal under the Ordinance, Article VI could not be considered an ex post facto law.

39. Major John Hamtramck to General Josiah Harmer, 29 July 1789 and 14 August 1789 in *Kaskaskia Records*, 506–8 and 508–9.

40. Bartholomew Tardiveau to Governor Arthur St. Clair, 30 June 1789, in Smith, ed., *St. Clair Papers*, 2:117–18.

41. Ibid.; Hamtramck to Harmer, 14 August 1789, *Kaskaskia Records*, 508–9.

42. *Journals of the Continental Congress*, 34:540–43, quotation at 541. Tardiveau wrote Governor St. Clair that privately a number of Congressmen "remarked that the intention of the obnoxious resolution had been solely to prevent the future importation of slaves into the Federal country; that it was not meant to affect the rights of the ancient inhabitants." Tardiveau to Governor St. Clair, 30 June 1789, *St. Clair Papers*, 2:117–18.

43. Governor Arthur St. Clair to President George Washington, 1 May 1790, in Clarence E. Carter, ed., *The Territorial Papers of the United States* (Washington, 1934), 2:244–48, quotation at 248.

44. "Report of Governor St. Clair to the Secretary of State [Thomas Jefferson]," 10 February 1791, *Territorial Papers*, 2:323–33.

45. St. Clair to Luke Deckar, 11 October 1793, *Territorial Papers*, 3: 415–16. The U.S. Supreme Court would make a similar analysis of a provision of the Mississippi Constitution of 1832, which prohibited the importation of slaves as merchandise. In *Groves v. Slaughter*, 15 Peters 449 (1841), the Court would assert that this provision could not become enforceable without legislative action.

46. Judge George Turner to Governor St. Clair, 14 June 1794, *St. Clair Papers*, 2:325–26; St. Clair to Turner, 14 December 1794, ibid., 330–32.

47. St. Clair to Winthrop Sargent, 28 April 1795, ibid., 340–42; "Inquiry into the Official Conduct of a Judge of the Supreme Court of the Northwest Territory," *American State Papers, Class X, Miscellaneous*, 1: 151–57; Governor St. Clair to William St. Clair, 3 June 1795, *St. Clair Papers*, 2:372–73.

48. These petitions are collected in Jacob P. Dunn, "Slavery Petitions and Papers," *Indiana Historical Society Publications* (Indianapolis, 1894), 2: 443–529. See also, "Slavery in the Indiana Territory," No. 222, 9th Congress, 2d Session, House of Representatives, *American State Papers, Miscellaneous*, 1:477–78; "Slavery in the Indiana Territory," No. 222, 10th Congress, 1st Session, Senate, *American State Papers, Miscellaneous*, 1:484–86; "Memorial of Randolph and St. Clair Counties, Jan. 17, 1806," ibid., 498; "Legislative Resolutions of 1807," ibid., 507; "Petition of Randolph and St. Clair Counties, Feb. 20, 1807," ibid., 521; "Legislative Petition of 1807," ibid., 515; and against slavery, "Petition of Randolph County, Feb. 20, 1807, "Counter to the Preceding Petition," ibid., 512; "Counter Petition of Clark County," ibid., 512; "Counter Petition of Clark County," ibid., 518; "Report on the Preceding," ibid., 521. "The Report of General W. Johnston, Chairman of the Committee to which the Petition on the Slavery Question had been Referred," reprinted from the *Vincennes Sun*, 17 December 1808, in ibid., 524.

49. "A Law concerning Servants. Adopted from the Virginia code, and published at Vincennes, the twenty-second day of September one thousand eight hundred and three,. . ." (hereinafter cited as "Law of 1803"), reprinted in Francis S. Philbrick, ed., *Laws of the Indiana Territory, 1801–1809* (Springfield, Ill., 1930), 42.

50. *The Address and Reply on the Presentation of a Testimonial to S. P. Chase, by the Colored People of Cincinnati* (Cincinnati, 1845), quoted at 12–13. For other arguments by Chase, see his *Speech of Salmon P. Chase, in the Case of the Colored Woman, Matilda, Who Was Brought Before Court of Common Pleas of Hamilton County, Ohio, by Writ of Habeas Corpus; March 11, 1837* (Cincinnati, 1837); *Birney v. The State*, 8 Ohio 230 (1837); and Chase, *Reclamation of Fugitives From Justice. An Argument for the Defendant, Submitted to the Supreme Court of the United States at the December Term, 1846, in the Case of Wharton Jones vs. John Van Zandt* (Cincinnati, 1847).

51. Poole, "Ordinance of 1787," 8–9.

52. *State v. Lasselle*, 1 Black. 60 (1820).

53. Harris, *History of Negro Servitude in Illinois*, 18; Glover Moore, *The Missouri Controversy, 1819–1821* (Lexington, 1953), 34, 54.

54. Illinois Constitution, 1818, Art. VI (declaring that slavery shall not "hereafter be introduced into this State," which implied that slaves

already in the state could be retained. This article also upheld certain forms of indentured servitude, and allowed slaves to be brought from other states for limited amounts of time to work in the salt making industry.)

55. For example, see *Hays v. Borders*, 1 Gilman (Illinois) 46 (1844) upholding indentures made before statehood that amounted to lifetime slavery. Illinois Constitution, 1848, Art. XIII, Sec. 16 finally abolished all slavery in the state.

56. Robert McColley, *Slavery and Jeffersonian Virginia*, 2d ed. (Urbana, 1973), argues that "What prevented the slaveholding planters from dominating Illinois and possibly Indiana, was, of all things, cotton," 181. McColley argues that cotton pulled slavery south, because that was where slavery was most profitable. This is a variation on the "natural limits" theory of slavery and is persuasive.

57. The number of slaves living in Indiana and Illinois is impossible to determine. The 1810 census listed 237 slaves and 393 free blacks in Indiana, "although many of the latter group were undoubtedly held under indentures." Thornbrough, *The Negro in Indiana*, 22. The 1820 census found 917 slaves in Illinois and 190 slaves in Indiana. Undoubtedly many of the 1,677 free blacks in those two states were also held in some form of servitude. As late as 1840 Illinois had 331 slaves. It is likely that more than 2,000 persons were held in slavery in Indiana and Illinois between 1787 and 1848.

V

The Development of Public Universities in the Old Northwest

JURGEN HERBST
Professor of Educational Policy Studies and History,
University of Wisconsin, Madison

Tradition and Revolution

THE NORTHWEST ORDINANCE OF JULY 13, 1787, and the Morrill Act of July 2, 1862, rank as the two most important documents in the history of the national government's influence over American higher education. That influence has been both traditional and revolutionary. It has been traditional in linking the nineteenth century experience of the American people to their European and colonial past. It has been revolutionary through curricular innovations and experiments that opened the doors of the country's universities to working men and women who never before had dreamed of enjoying the benefits of higher education.

When in the Northwest Ordinance the members of the Congress of the Confederation wrote that "religion, morality, and knowledge, being necessary to good government and the happiness of mankind, schools and the means of education shall forever be encouraged," they expressed their concern that government assume a measure of responsibility for the support of higher education.[1] In doing so they followed long standing tradition. Throughout the colonial period crown, royal governors, and provincial legislatures acted upon the Reformation legacy that secular government and established church were jointly responsible for the establishment, protection, and survival—though not necessarily for the full financial support—of the colleges in their realm.

Such responsibility had been first assumed in 1636 by the General Court of the Massachusetts Bay Colony with its pledge of £400 for what was to become Harvard College. It was asserted again just before and during the Revolution when in 1775 the New Hampshire Assembly gave Dartmouth College a grant of £560, and when in 1775 and 1776 the Continental Congress added $500 each year and $925 in 1778 in recognition of the college's role in helping defend and pacify the frontier. New Hampshire's largesse did not cease after the war either. In 1784 and 1787 the state authorized lotteries, in 1790 it appropriated funds, and in 1791 it granted land to the college. Even Vermont joined in, and in 1785 gave Dartmouth a grant of 23,000 acres. The members of the Confederation Congress followed well-worn footpaths.[2]

The authors of the Northwest Ordinance were as concerned with their responsibility for the future as they were mindful of the actions of colonial governments in the past. By 1787 it was already becoming obvious that attitudes towards higher education were changing. Americans had caught "college enthusiasm," as Ezra Stiles had reported from Newport, Rhode Island, in 1770, where he had learned of plans for new college foundations in New Hampshire, Georgia, South Carolina, and Rhode Island.[3] Within the following seventeen years two colleges had been chartered in Maryland, two in Virginia, one in what was to become Kentucky, two in Pennsylvania, one in Georgia, and three in South Carolina. Of these eleven foundations only one, the University of Georgia, could be considered a state institution. All the rest owed their existence to denominational, local, or joint state-denominational initiatives.[4] Colleges, it appeared, were being founded with the interest of particular groups in mind. Was there a need to ensure that the people of the new states as a whole would be well served by higher education?

The members of the Congress of the Confederation had other reasons to be concerned. The enthusiasm for college founding by denominational and civic groups reflected a growing dissatisfaction with the aristocratic temper of the colonial colleges. Americans felt alienated from colleges in which a privileged few were groomed for influential positions in government, church, and society. They disliked the classical curriculum with its emphasis on Latin, a subject that they felt did not help them in their daily task and concerns. Thus in many states they came to favor common and preparatory schools over the colleges. As John Whitehead has pointed out, it was only in South Carolina and Virginia, states which did not actively support their common schools, that appropriations for the universities continued.[5] Happy to throw off the burden of the colonial past, ordinary Americans opted for local educational institutions that responded to their desire for practical, down-to-earth education. They were quite willing for the colleges to fend for themselves.

The concern for higher education as a public commitment on state and national levels, however, survived in the Confederation Congress and among a small band of revolutionary statesmen. It found expression in the several proposals submitted to Congress for a national university as well as in the plans to regulate the sale and settlement of western lands. The Ordinance of 1787 wedded these concerns to the desire of New England settlers to find in their new homes educational institutions for their children. The sales contract between the Ohio Company and the Board of Treasury, signed on October 27, 1787, incorporated these sentiments in an enforceable legal document that explicitly referred to two townships "to be given perpetually for the purposes of an university. . . ."[6] A precedent was set that remained a potent example for subsequent legislation under the Federal Constitution of 1789.

As developments in the nineteenth century would show, the revolutionary power of the sentiments expressed in the Northwest Ordinance left their most enduring imprint on religious and curricular matters. Federal support for higher education encouraged those who, like Jefferson, opposed the spread of sectarianism and religious bigotry in higher education. It reminded Americans that they could ill afford to let their common commitment to republican principles and democratic procedures be undermined by sectarian rivalry and intolerance.

In curricular matters, it was above all the generosity of the Congress as expressed in the Morrill Act of 1862 that permitted and prodded state governments to supplement the efforts of traditional liberal arts colleges with novel departures in agricultural, mechanical, and teacher education. Already in the antebellum decades the proportion of both younger and older students had been larger in midwestern states than in other regions. The younger students crowded into the preparatory departments, and the older ones availed themselves of the opportunities for scientific and vocational preparation.[7] Yet the full effects of the Morrill Act did not become apparent until the century's end. The act showed that a nation could place the responsibility for higher education in the hands of popularly elected representatives without succumbing to the centrifugal and self-seeking forces of individual and group self-interest. The results proved that Americans knew how to recognize, protect, and advance the common welfare.

Precarious Beginnings

The history of the first public universities incorporated under the provisions of the Northwest Ordinance and the Ohio Company contract illustrate the fragility of public institutions in a frontier society. Everywhere *laissez-faire* became the rule of the day. Colleges were founded for a wide variety of reasons: private promoters and city officials sought to attract settlers; churches were intent upon saving the frontier from barbarism and atheism; professionals hoped to establish proprietary law and medical schools to augment their incomes and train their successors. Few showed enthusiasm to support state institutions with tax levies.

In Ohio the two public universities remained the state's stepchildren. The Ohio University at Athens, originally incorporated as the American Western University on January 2, 1802, and rechartered under its new name on February 18, 1804, was directed by trustees who were selected and could be replaced only by the legislature itself. Even though the governor served on the board ex officio, however, the legislature did no more than enforce the collections of taxes owed the university on its lands. In 1843 legislators made matters worse when, ignoring the increasing market value of these lands, they disallowed their re-evaluation. The Miami University at Oxford, chartered on February 17, 1809, received its first financial support from the state when the legislature agreed to pay the tuition fees of Civil War veterans. While the Ohio University had to wait until 1877 for its first state appropriation, annual state payments for Miami only began in 1885. Not until 1896 did Miami share the state mill levy with its sister institution in Athens.[8]

In Indiana, too, the state's institution for higher education had to learn to live within its income from land sales and from tuition payments. Originally chartered by the territorial legislature as Vincennes University on November 29, 1806, it was to admit Indian children and, with the help of a lottery, open a college for women students. The expected funds, however, failed to materialize, and only a grammar school operated from 1811 to 1818. This school was reopened in 1823 and became known as the Knox County Seminary.

Vincennes University itself had never opened its doors.[9] Reincorporated as the Indiana Seminary at Bloomington on January 20, 1820, it was rechristened eight years later as Indiana College, only to be re-named Indiana University in 1838. It took twenty-nine more years for the legislature to make its first direct grant. Even then the annual appropriations remained small when compared with state grants to and private incomes of eastern institutions.[10]

The early state institutions in Ohio and Indiana felt the financial neglect they suffered at the hands of their legislators even more as people generally favored the colleges of their own denomination and accused the state institutions of being in their very nature "less attentive to religion and good morals. . . than other seminaries established by particular denominations."[11] This charge hurt all the more as it was manifestly untrue. At both Ohio and Miami universities the early presidents and many faculty members had been or-dained Presbyterian ministers. Many trustees were Presbyterian laymen. Not until 1885 did Miami choose a lay president. As the college historian wrote: "Though Miami University was created by the Federal Congress and established by the State of Ohio, it could not have been more Presbyterian if founded by John Knox. . . . From the start Miami had been . . . the principal training ground of Presbyterian ministers in Ohio."[12]

Given denominational loyalties most Ohioans apparently saw no reason why they should support their two public universities at Athens and Oxford in preference to the state's twelve denominational schools.[13] Their legislature also did not hesitate in 1836 to grant small sums to two nonreligious private schools. In one of these it claimed the right to appoint the trustees.[14] Clearly, the two state universities were justified in feeling overlooked and discriminated against.

In Indiana we encounter the same story. Here, too, the pervasive denominational loyalties of the people stood as an obstacle to popular support of the state university. Indiana University's historian observed correctly that "yearly decisions of the Assembly clearly showed that the legislators could not differentiate between schools organized to serve narrow sectarian objectives and the broader based public university which served as a liberal arts and professional institution."[15] In addition, the adherence of the faculty to a traditional college curriculum prompted legislators to ask why they should grant funds to the university that they were not expected to give to the sectarian schools? They rejected the assertion of the school's first instructor, classicist and Presbyterian minister Baynard Rush Hall, that grammar school and traditional college subjects taught in an atmosphere of close disciplinary supervision were "the best *intellectual* education for both rich and poor."[16]

When Andrew Wylie, the next president and another Presbyterian clergyman, reaffirmed the primacy of classical studies, moral instruction, and the *in loco parentis* role of the faculty, and eschewed the practical studies called for by some of Indiana's pioneer settlers, the legislature demanded that the University introduce studies in law, engineering, and military science. Trustees, president, and faculty, however, refused to comply because the legislature appeared unwilling to fund the new programs. By 1842 only a part-time professor of law had taken up his duties.[17]

The same faculty resistance appeared during the 1850s when the legislature, without granting the necessary funds, pressed the university to begin instruction in agriculture, engineering, and education. The decade of the Civil War only made matters worse, and the crowning blow came in 1869 when the legislature refused to give the Morrill Land Grant funds to Indiana University. At that point all hopes were gone that the university might become the state's primary institution offering instruction in every area demanded by its citizens. Indiana University was now thrown back almost entirely on the liberal arts.[18]

In both Ohio and Indiana the situation was the same.

President William Henry Scott of Ohio University summed it up well in his lament of 1875: "We have called to the State to bestow some care on the eldest-born of all our institutions, but she has paid no heed."[19] Denominational rivalries and faculty conservatism were the disabling defects of the early state universities.

The Second Wave

When the next generation of state universities opened their doors to students, the outlook for pubic institutions had become more favorable. In what was to become the state of Michigan, the university—modelled in 1817 on the University of France and fancifully named the "Catholepistemiad"—was the first institution of higher education to exist, at least on paper. It was to be a system of public instruction including common schools, academies, colleges, and a university proper.[20] In Wisconsin, where the university was to be located "at or near the seat of state government," there, too, was little competition from private colleges.[21] Its regents declared that "by making our University the *school of the schoolmaster*" they intended "to make . . . [it] subsidiary to the great cause of popular education. . . . "[22]

In both states university pioneers sought hard to avoid the accusations of sectarianism and godlessness. The Michigan regents agreed that a strictly observed non-sectarianism should guide their decisions, but they expected students to attend daily chapel and a church of their choice on Sundays. For their professorial appointments they chose a Methodist, a Baptist, a Presbyterian, and an Episcopalian clergyman. They refused to name a university president, and arranged instead that the professors representing the four major denominations take turns presiding for a year over the faculty.[23]

In Wisconsin the delegates to the Constitutional Convention of 1847/1848 had explicitly forbidden sectarian instruction at the new institution. But they may have been too optimistic if they had hoped to escape the familiar accusations of godlessness. The supporters of the denominational colleges distrusted the state university on principle. When the university celebrated its opening in Madison on January 1850 with a formal inauguration ball, a professor at the nearby Congregational college in Beloit wrote to a friend that the ball had forced him to expect "to find the University an actual opponent to Christian education." Five years later an attempt by the assembly to divert part of the income from the university fund to the denominational colleges showed that the "godless" image was hard to overcome.[24]

When in 1841 and 1849 respectively the first students enrolled in Ann Arbor and in Madison the needs of a pioneer population for instruction in both academic and practical fields guided early plans. The university at Ann Arbor was to consist of three departments: literature, science, and the arts; medicine; and law. To prepare students for entry public secondary schools were opened as university branches at seven locations in the state.[25] In Wisconsin the legislature ordered the regents to oversee the creation of the same three departments, but added the theory and practice of elementary instruction.[26] Michigan and Wisconsin wanted to make sure that their universities be spared the accusations of an outmoded curriculum.

Initially, the Michigan regents could be quite satisfied with their results. Though their early program reflected the traditional emphasis on the classics—the medical and law schools existed only on paper—the students at Ann Arbor received vigorous instruction in botany, zoology, geology, chemistry, and French. The first eleven graduates who were granted their bachelor's degrees in 1845, could be proud of the scientific training they had been given.

Matters improved even more with the election of Henry Tappan to the presidency in 1852. Tappan was familiar with the German universities and advocated the enlargement of the library, the establishment of laboratories, the substitution of lectures for recitations, and greater emphasis on research. His professional appointments brought in science teachers from the military academy at West Point and additional professors of medicine. He installed an observatory, awarded the first bachelor of science and of civil engineering degrees, and inaugurated graduate work taken in course. By 1857 the university had grown to 287 students in the literary department and 173 in the medical school. Two years later instruction in law began. Within another two years the regents reported that the law department and the chemical laboratory were, each in its own field, the largest of any in the country.[27] The Wisconsin regents, however, were not quite so lucky. Already in 1850 a newspaper had taken the "stall-fed denizens of Madison" to task for their preference for training doctors, lawyers, and ministers. "If the friends of this literary hierarchy wish to find favor for it in the eyes of those who will be compelled to support it," the paper editorialized, "let them make it an institution that shall be useful to the masses . . . and establish those departments which shall be open for the farmer and mechanic. . . ."[28]

The regents were quite willing to do that and sent their president to Ann Arbor for information and advice. During the next few years they published plans for the establishment of various university departments and, in 1856, they announced the beginnings of instruction in the application of science to the arts. In the same year a department of medicine was begun and plans laid for the law department. There was talk also of teaching engineering, physics, astronomy, and commerce.

However laudable these moves, they failed to quiet complaints in the press and legislature that, as one assembly committee put it, the university did "not occupy its true educational position." The crux of the matter was, as a second committee added, "our State University does not materially vary from our ordinary

college in the course of study pursued." In that observation the legislators were confirmed by the university's
professor of chemistry and natural history who was to
refer derisively to the university's "curriculum of fossil
usages" and to his colleagues as "fossil men who are
subject to hydrophobic spasms at the mere mention of
the word science."[29]

By 1857 dissatisfaction with the university had
reached such proportions that the legislature passed a
law appropriating income from the swamp land fund to
the support of teacher training in colleges and academies while deliberately excluding the university. Instead, a board of normal school regents was created that
rivaled the university regents. For a brief period an
attempt was made to bridge the gap between the two
boards with Henry Barnard's appointment as both
chancellor of the university and agent for the state's
normal school regents. But his presence could not stem
the distrust of the university and the growing conviction
that teacher training was better left to separate normal
schools.[30]

In Michigan as well as in Wisconsin the universities'
problems lay less with a supposed unwillingness of faculties and presidents to engage in new and practical
studies than with uncertainty on nearly everybody's part
how best to do this. In 1863 the Michigan regents
dismissed President Tappan despite his success in dem-
onstrating just what a modern state university could
achieve and how it could serve its society best.[31] Tappan
lost his battle chiefly because he failed to convince
Michigan settlers that he understood their situation and
needs. By the early 1860s neither he nor his academic
colleagues at Ann Arbor and Madison had found a way
to respond to the ever-repeated demands for a higher
education appropriate to the lives of farmers and mechanics. They had as yet been unable to forge a bridge
between the traditional liberal and professional education and the rising demand for practical studies in the
sciences applied to agriculture and mechanics. Would

their successors in the states' public institutions succeed
in that enterprise?

New Departures: The Single Purpose Institutions

For attempts to answer that question contemporaries
need only have looked to other academic experiments
conducted in Michigan and Illinois. In 1853 the Michigan State Normal School opened its doors in Ypsilanti,
and four years later instruction began at the Agricultural College of the State of Michigan in East Lansing. In Illinois, the State Normal University opened its
doors in Normal in the same year. The founders of these
institutions had given up on the dream of a comprehensive state university in which the traditional preparatory and professional subjects as well as the new, practical skills were taught side by side. Instead they created
separate institutions that were free of the taint of "fossil
men and fossil subjects" and devoted themselves single-
mindedly to training teachers, farmers, and mechanics.

Michigan's State Normal School, financed with congressional saline land funds and chartered on March 28,
1849, prepared men and women teachers for both elementary and secondary schools through pre-collegiate
vocational training. The school remained at that level
until in 1890 it conferred its first bachelor of pedagogics
degrees.[32] The Agricultural College in East Lansing, on
the other hand, promising to offer instruction beneficial
to farmers and others interested in the application of
science to practical pursuits, from the start offered a
four-year curriculum of the liberal arts and sciences.[33]

Not surprisingly, the college at East Lansing found
itself in the familiar crossfire of debate. President, faculty, and friends in the state's agricultural society
strongly backed the academic program and the requirement that students earn their keep through manual
labor. That latter requirement consisted of clearing the
forest and working the college farm. It served no educa-

tional purpose beyond practicing such specialized skills as tree pruning and laying drain tile.[34] Opposition, however, arose to the liberal arts program in the legislature and the board of education. The faculty and the agricultural society prevailed, however, and a four-year curriculum was adopted that placed heavy emphasis on the liberal arts, the sciences, and such practical subjects as engineering, surveying, technology, and household economy. The first graduates left the institution in 1861 with their bachelor degrees in hand.[35]

The State Agricultural College showed that faculty, students, and supporters of a school founded for the express purpose of agricultural education would find it in their own interest to seek a solid foundation in liberal and scientific studies.[36] But the college did not offer instruction in agriculture itself. Why this curious omission? The answer was the same as we have found in Ann Arbor and Madison. The faculty lacked scientific knowledge and established teaching materials. These had to be created first.

The real pioneering work of the State Agricultural College took place during the 1850s and 1860s in its laboratories and on its experimental fields. The college garnered a reputation for its research scholars and, in subsequent decades, for their interest in what came to be called outreach and extension work with farmers and agricultural societies. Its students made their mark in many scientific and nonscientific fields, agriculture being only one among many. By 1885 40 percent of its graduates had been trained for and had gone into farming. That was a far higher percentage than that achieved at the state universities.[37]

In Illinois the State Normal University represented a great alliance of all of Illinois' various social factions and educational interests that had felt neglected by the traditional colleges. Their battle had brought together the supporters of Jonathan Turner's campaign for an industrial university, the friends of agricultural education, and the advocates of a state normal school.[38]

Their strategy was to combine the practical fields in a new, state-supported university rather than to offer them each in an institution of its own. But the reality of the institution was to differ from that vision. The deliberate use of the term university could not hide the fact that throughout the nineteenth century the institution remained a normal school. As State Superintendent William H. Powell had explained in 1859, the term normal university instead of normal school was to ensure that, should the people of Illinois demand it in the future, the institution could be "swelled into the full proportions of a university. . . ."[39] But that did not happen until 1908 when the Normal University granted its first bachelor degree and when, in 1963, it became the Illinois State University.

In the Old Northwest, then, the Agricultural College of the State of Michigan can take credit for having first tackled the problem of learning how to combine a traditional liberal arts education with scientific laboratory instruction and experimental work. This was its way of responding to the need for applied scientific training in practical tasks. The single-purpose state college devoted to applying science to practical tasks of everyday life, rather than the encompassing state university, first tackled one of the most vexing problems of nineteenth century higher education: to provide proof that public support for public institutions of higher education was justified by the contributions these institutions could make to popular education.

The Comprehensive State Universities

The final step in assuring that the American people would succeed in creating colleges and universities that served wide sections of the work population in many different fields came in 1862 when the Congress responded favorably to petitions received from several states and to the repeated initiatives of Senator Justin

Morrill from Vermont. It provided 30,000 acres for each congressman and senator to states that would establish agricultural and mechanical colleges.[40]

Of the states carved out of the Northwest Territory Michigan and Wisconsin assigned the Morrill land-grants to existing institutions. In Michigan the success of the State Agricultural College at East Lansing as a single purpose institution virtually assured that it was chosen as the beneficiary of the Morrill grant. To be sure, there were attempts to incorporate the college into the university at Ann Arbor, but the strength of farming interests in the legislature prevented any such schemes. In Wisconsin the university regents and the legislature quickly agreed that, in the absence of a separate agricultural school, the university at Madison would be the logical choice.

But in the three other states new institutions were planned. In Illinois, Indiana, and Ohio the legislatures became jousting grounds for competing interests. The struggle pitched the supporters of the denominational colleges against the spokesmen for industrial-mechanical and agricultural education. Friends of existing institutions battled advocates of new foundations. When the dust settled, the Illinois Industrial University had been born. It opened its doors in 1868 at Champaign-Urbana. Two years later it announced the beginning of a school of agriculture with a curriculum of its own, borrowing heavily from the instruction offered already in the science course. In the other two states the debates ended in stalemate. In Indiana the offer of land and endowment funds from a wealthy businessman led to the incorporation of Purdue University in 1869 and its opening in Lafayette five years later. In Ohio, where the struggle had involved the two state institutions at Athens and Oxford as well as other parties, the deadlock was broken by chartering in 1870 the Ohio Agricultural and Mechanical College at Columbus.

How did the various states cope with the new opportunities offered by the Morrill Act? Would their new institutions succeed in offering quality education in agriculture, mechanics, and the liberal arts? As we have already discussed the prominent role of research and the liberal arts program at the Michigan State Agricultural College, so it is perhaps not surprising to note that in East Lansing little was heard of instruction in mechanics. The college's backers continued to insist that agricultural education was its sole function. Yet by 1888 the college did grant its first engineering degrees, and by 1910 civil and electrical engineering were well established at East Lansing.[41]

Wisconsin encountered a familiar problem. Though the regents were willing to start a school of agriculture, they were unable to find students eager to enroll. By 1878 the school could boast of just one graduate. Three years later the *Wisconsin Journal of Education* reported that while only one student was enrolled in agriculture, sixty were studying law.[42] Wisconsin's farm organizations lost their patience. In 1884 a farmers' convention demanded the establishment of an independent agricultural college. The regents responded by literally forcing the university's professor of agriculture to develop vocational short courses of agricultural instruction through farmers' institutes away from the campus. Agricultural instruction in Wisconsin became a reality when it moved off-campus and supplemented the research and experimentation program carried on in Madison.[43]

The lesson learned in Wisconsin was that a state university could not expect the continuing support of its people if it intended only to teach its students on campus. It had to address itself directly to the economic and social problems of the people in their communities. This is what the farmers' institutes and the short courses began to do.[44] The result was a slowly increasing appreciation of the university by the people of the state. "The cold indifference. . .," the regents remarked in 1889, "has given place to an earnest solicitude and deep interest in the welfare of the University. . . . The people have come to look upon it as their university and to rejoice to see it taking rank with the first educational institutions of the country."[45] In Wisconsin's neighbor to the south the university trustees, among whom farmers constituted the largest occupational group, insisted that the school avoid the failings of an old-time college, and breathe an air of modernity and practicality. As the university's historian noted, they wanted the institution to be "a center of utilitarian education for the producing classes."[46] But John Milton Gregory, the university's president, read the Morrill Act to mean that instruction in the practical sciences of agriculture and industry required a thorough training in literary and scientific culture. The university's graduates were to be prepared to fulfill their functions as citizens and professionals as well as their peers in the traditional learned professions.

The ensuing conflicts and debates were complicated by the problem of attracting students to agricultural education. Faced with the absence of a scientific agricultural curriculum, Gregory endorsed the ideas of Justus von Liebig in Germany where agricultural and polytechnic schools were joined to the other faculties of the universities. He also promoted experimental farming and direct involvement of the university with the farmers of the state through off-campus lectures and institutes. These initiatives took time to take root and showed their results only in the 1880s.[47]

The mechanical and engineering curriculum, on the other hand, fared better. Here the Illinois Industrial University succeeded early in stimulating its students to become productive in research and invention as well as in practical engineering tasks. By 1873 the university offered a full program in its colleges of agriculture, engineering, natural science, and literature and science.[48] Gregory had managed to bring the university into the modern age. Under his tutelage it offered its students a wide and free choice of fields to study, embracing the full breadth of subjects the Morrill Act had proposed. If the spokesmen for the agrarian interests felt neglected, it was only because they sought an exclusive emphasis on their field.

Indiana and Ohio faced similar problems. The lack of prepared students and of experience in teaching applied science and the hostility of denominational and agricultural interests towards a broadly based liberal arts and scientific-engineering program hindered development. At Columbus, the grant of state appropriations was delayed until 1877. With the impetus supplied by the Hatch Act ten years later and the Second Morrill Act of 1890, Purdue's agricultural and mechanical instruction began to flourish. Ohio's agricultural interests also received their due so that a broad-based course could be charted that would promise fulfillment of the early dreams for a comprehensive state university.[49]

One hundred and three years had passed between the signing of the Northwest Ordinance and the Second Morrill Act. Throughout this time the congressional commitment to the encouragement of "schools and the means of education" had buoyed the aspirations and stiffened the determination of Americans who sought to open colleges and universities to men and women of all classes, occupations, and professions. After a little more than a century, American higher education had been radically altered. No longer was it the exclusive domain of a professional class restricted to lawyers, physicians, ministers, magistrates, and scholars. Now farmers and engineers, men and women of all walks of life who sought a college education and scientific and vocational training found open doors at their state universities and colleges. What is more, the institutions themselves, their investigators, scholars, and teachers, had learned how to address themselves to new problems and new tasks in research and teaching. The traditional liberal arts and sciences and instruction in their practical applications, scientific research, and outreach and extension found a common home in America's land grant colleges and universities. The farsightedness and generosity of

Congress expressed in the Northwest Ordinance and the Morrill and Hatch Acts had made this possible.

---

1. For the text of the Ordinance see William E. Peters, *Legal History of the Ohio University* (Cincinnati, 1910), 30–38.

2. On the relationship of government to colleges during the colonial period see my *From Crisis to Crisis: American College Government, 1636–1819* (Cambridge, 1982), passim. Governments shared their responsibility for higher education with churches and communities. They did not have to wait for a "rising secularism and the separation of church and state" to be "freed" to support education, as Winton Solberg indicates. See Solberg, *The University of Illinois, 1867–1894: An Intellectual and Cultural History* (Urbana, 1968), 5.

3. Franklin B. Dexter, ed., *The Literary Diary of Ezra Stiles* (New York, 1901), 1:45–46.

4. Washington College and St. John's in Maryland and Transylvania in Kentucky were joint state-denominational ventures; the College of Charleston was a public municipal foundation. Six institutions were sponsored and supported as denominational enterprises without any official state involvement. Five of these—Liberty Hall and Hampden-Sydney in Virginia, Dickinson in Pennsylvania, and Mount Sion and the College of Cambridge in South Carolina—were guided by Presbyterians, and one—Franklin in Pennsylvania—jointly by German Reformed and German Lutheran congregations.

5. John Whitehead, *The Separation of College and State* (New Haven, 1973), 140. See also, Norman K. Risjord, *Chesapeake Politics 1781–1800* (New York, 1978), 214–15, and Samuel Knox' 1797 essay in Frederick Rudolph, ed., *Essays on Education in the Early Republic* (Cambridge, 1965), 275–76, 285.

6. See the text of the sales contract in Peters, *Legal History of the Ohio University*, 43–48. See also George N. Rainsford, *Congress and Higher Education in the Nineteenth Century* (Knoxville, 1972), 36–39.

7. See Colin B. Burke, *American Collegiate Populations: A Test of the Traditional View* (New York, 1982), 126–36.

8. Richard Rees Price, *The Financial Support of State Universities* (Cambridge, 1924), 79; Walter Havighurst, *The Miami Years 1809–1969* (New York, 1969), 140, 160; Thomas N. Hoover, *The History of Ohio University* (Athens, 1954), 161.

9. See Howard R. Burnett, "Early History of Vincennes University," *Indiana Magazine of History* 29 (June 1933): 114–21.

10. Thomas D. Clark, *Indiana University: Midwestern Pioneer* (Bloomington, 1970–1977), 1:198–99; Price, *The Financial Support of State Universities*, 90.

11. Hoover, *The History of Ohio University*, 65.

12. Havighurst, *The Miami Years 1809–1969*, 46, 103.

13. The twelve denominational colleges in Ohio were Episcopal Kenyon, Congregational Western Reserve, Marietta, and Oberlin, Presbyterian Muskingum, Methodist Wesleyan and Mount Union, Lutheran Wittenberg, Brethren Otterbein, Baptist Granville (later Denison), German Reformed Heidelberg, and Catholic St. Xavier.

14. Edward Alanson Miller, *The History of Educational Legislation in Ohio from 1803 to 1850* (New York, 1969), 92. The two schools were the College of Ripley in Brown County and Franklin College in Harrison County. Neither of them appears to have survived for any length of time.

15. Clark, *Indiana University: Midwestern Pioneer*, 1:79, 150, 201. By mid-century Indiana's seven denominational institutions and their years of incorporation were Presbyterian Hanover College (1833) and Wabash College (1934), Baptist Franklin College (1836), Methodist Indiana Asbury (1837), (later called DePauw University), Lutheran Concordia College (1839), and the Catholic University of Notre Dame (1842) as well as Saint Mary's Academy (1844).

16. Ibid. 1:32.

17. On President Wylie's reign see ibid. 1:49–77.

18. Ibid. 1:79, 95, 115–16.

19. Hoover, *The History of Ohio University*, 146.

20. Howard H. Peckham, *The Making of The University of Michigan, 1817–1967* (Ann Arbor, 1967), 5–9.

21. In Michigan what was to become Kalamazoo College in 1855 had been a "literary institute" when the university was chartered. In 1840 it became one of the university's branches. What was later to become Albion College was the Wesleyan Seminary at Albion when the university admitted its first students. In Wisconsin only Carroll College and Beloit College existed as colleges when the university was chartered.

22. Merle Curti and Vernon Carstensen, *The University of Wisconsin: A History, 1848–1925* (Madison, 1949), 1:49, 74.

23. Peckham, *The Making of The University of Michigan*, 19, 23; Willis F. Dunbar, *The Michigan Record in Higher Education* (Detroit, 1963), 69.

24. Curti and Carstensen, *The University of Wisconsin*, 1:63n, 88.

25. Peckham, *The Making of The University of Michigan*, 16, 19, 20, 22. The seven university branches were located in Pontiac, Detroit, Monroe, Kalamazoo, Niles, Tecumseh, and White Pigeon.

26. Curti and Carstensen, *The University of Wisconsin*, 1:49–50, 53.

27. Peckham, *The Making of The University of Michigan*, 31–44, passim.

28. Editorial, *Southport Telegraph*, 15 February 1850.

29. Curti and Carstensen, *The University of Wisconsin*, 1:72–79, 94n, 99, 100.

30. Ibid. 1:92, 108, 113.

31. Peckham, *The Making of The University of Michigan*, 31–52.

32. Egbert R. Isbell, *A History of Eastern Michigan University, 1849–1965* (Ypsilanti, 1971), 1–29.

33. Dunbar, *The Michigan Record in Higher Education*, 85, 86.

34. Madison Kuhn, *Michigan State: The First Hundred Years, 1855–1955* (East Lansing, 1955), 26–27.

35. Ibid., 62–64.

36. Ibid., 26.

37. Ibid., 118–19.

38. Helen E. Marshall, *Grandest of Enterprises: Illinois State Normal University, 1857–1957* (Normal, 1956), 3–16.

39. Ibid., 18.

40. Rainsford, *Congress and Higher Education*, 46–97, passim.

41. Dunbar, *The Michigan Record in Higher Education*, 233–34; Kuhn, *Michigan State*, 146–50.

42. Curti and Carstensen, *The University of Wisconsin*, 1:461–63, 464.

43. Wilbur H. Glover, "The Agricultural College Crisis of 1885," *Wisconsin Magazine of History*, 32 (September 1948): 17–25.

44. Wilbur H. Glover, *Farm and College: The College of Agriculture of the University of Wisconsin* (Madison, 1952), 112–32.

45. Regents' Executive Committee, June 1889, quoted in Curti and Carstensen, *The University of Wisconsin*, 1:586.

46. Solberg, *The University of Illinois, 1867–1894*, 81–83; Harry A. Kersey, Jr., *John Milton Gregory and the University of Illinois* (Urbana, 1968), 106–8.

47. Ibid.

48. Ibid., 122.

49. William Murray Hepburn and Louis Martin Sears, *Purdue University: Fifty Years of Progress* (Indianapolis, 1925), 77, 91; William A. Kinnison, *Building Sullivant's Pyramid: An Administrative History of the Ohio State University, 1870–1907* (Columbus, 1970), passim.

APPENDIX

An Ordinance for the government of the territory of the United States North West of the river Ohio.[1]

BE IT ORDAINED BY THE UNITED STATES IN CON-gress Assembled that the said territory for the purposes of temporary government be one district, subject how-ever to be divided into two districts as future circum-stances may in the Opinion of Congress make it expe-dient.

Be it ordained by the authority aforesaid, that the estates both of resident and non resident proprietors in the said territory dying intestate shall descend to and be distributed among their children and the descendants of a deceased child in equal parts; the descendants of a deceased child or grandchild to take the share of their deceased parent in equal parts among them; and where there shall be no children or descendants then in equal parts to the next of kin in equal degree and among collaterals the children of a deceased brother or sister of the intestate shall have in equal parts among them their deceased parent's share and there shall in no case be a distinction between kindred of the whole and half blood; saving in all cases to the widow of the intestate her third

---

[1]Roscoe R. Hill, ed., *Journals of the Continental Congress, 1774-1789,* vol. 32 (Washington, D.C., 1936), 334–43. Except for the editor's cita-tions, which have been deleted, the text has not been altered. The underscored portions of the Ordinance were added during the debate on 13 July 1787.

part of the real estate for life, and one third part of the personal estate; and this law relative to descents and dower shall remain in full force until altered by the legislature of the district. And until the governor and judges shall adopt laws as hereinafter mentioned estates in the said territory may be devised or bequeathed by wills in writing signed and sealed by him or her in whom the estate may be, being of full age, and attested by three witnesses, and real estates may be conveyed by lease and release or bargain and sale signed, sealed and delivered by the person being of full age in whom the estate may be and attested by two witnesses provided such wills be duly proved and such conveyances be acknowledged or the execution thereof duly proved and be recorded within one year after proper magistrates, courts and registers shall be appointed for that purpose and personal property may be transferred by delivery saving however to the french and canadian inhabitants and other settlers of the Kaskaskies, Saint Vincents and the neighbouring villages who have heretofore professed themselves citizens of Virginia, their laws and customs now in force among them relative to the descent and conveyance of property.

Be it ordained by the authority aforesaid that there shall be appointed from time to time by Congress a governor, whose commission shall continue in force for the term of three years, unless sooner revoked by Congress; he shall reside in the district and have a freehold estate therein, in one thousand acres of land while in the exercise of his office. There shall be appointed from time to time by Congress a secretary, whose commission shall continue in force for four years, unless sooner revoked; he shall reside in the district and have a freehold estate therein in five hundred acres of land while in the exercise of his office; It shall be his duty to keep and preserve the acts and laws passed by the legislature and the public records of the district and the proceedings of the governor in his executive department and transmit authentic copies of such acts and proceedings every six months to the Secretary of Congress. There shall also be appointed a court to consist of three judges any two of whom to form a court, who shall have a common law jurisdiction and reside in the district and have each therein a freehold estate in five hundred acres of land while in the exercise of their offices, and their commissions shall continue in force during good behaviour.

The governor, and judges or a majority of them shall adopt and publish in the district such laws of the original states criminal and civil as may be necessary and best suited to the circumstances of the district and report them to Congress from time to time, which laws shall be in force in the district until the organization of the general assembly therein, unless disapproved of by Congress; but afterwards the legislature shall have authority to alter them as they shall think fit.

The governor for the time being shall be Commander in chief of the militia, appoint and commission all officers in the same below the rank of general Officers; All general Officers shall be appointed and commissioned by Congress.

Previous to the Organization of the general Assembly the governor shall appoint such magistrates and other civil officers in each county or township, as he shall find necessary for the preservation of the peace and good order in the same. After the general Assembly shall be organized, the powers and duties of magistrates and other civil officers shall be regulated and defined by the said Assembly; but all magistrates and other civil officers, not herein otherwise directed shall during the continuance of this temporary government be appointed by the governor.

For the prevention of crimes and injuries the laws to be adopted or made shall have force in all parts of the district and for the execution of process criminal and civil, the governor shall make proper divisions thereof, and he shall proceed from time to time as circumstances may require to lay out the parts of the district in which the indian titles shall have been extinguished into counties and townships subject however to such alterations as may thereafter be made by the legislature.

So soon as there shall be five thousand free male inhabitants of full age in the district upon giving proof thereof to the governor, they shall receive authority with time and place to elect representatives from their counties or townships to represent them in the general assembly, provided that for every five hundred free male inhabitants there shall be one representative and so on progressively with the number of free male inhabitants shall the right of representation encrease until the number of representatives shall amount to twenty five after which the number and proportion of representatives shall be regulated by the legislature; provided that no person be eligible or qualified to act as a representative unless he shall have been a citizen of one of the United States three years and be a resident in the district or unless he shall have resided in the district three years and in either case shall likewise hold in his own right in fee simple two hundred acres of land within the same; provided also that a freehold in fifty acres of land in the district having been a citizen of one of the states and being resident in the district; or the like freehold and two years residence in the district shall be necessary to qualify a man as an elector of a representative.

The representatives thus elected shall serve for the term of two years and in case of the death of a representative or removal from office, the governor shall issue a writ to the county or township for which he was a member, to elect another in his stead to serve for the residue of the term.

The general assembly or legislature shall consist of the governor, legislative council and a house of representatives. The legislative council shall consist of five members to continue in Office five years unless sooner removed by Congress any three of whom to be a quorum and the members of the council shall be nominated and appointed in the following manner, to wit; As soon as representatives shall be elected, the governor shall appoint a time and place for them to meet together, and when met they shall nominate ten persons residents in the district and each possessed of a freehold in five hundred acres of Land and return their names to Congress; five of whom Congress shall appoint and commission to serve as aforesaid; and whenever a vacancy shall happen in the council by death or removal from office, the house of representatives shall nominate two persons qualified as aforesaid, for each vacancy, and return their names to Congress, one of whom Congress shall appoint and commission for the residue of the term, and every five years, four months at least before the expiration of the time of service of the Members of Council, the said house shall nominate ten persons qualified as aforesaid, and return their names to Congress, five of whom Congress shall appoint and commission to serve as Members of the council five years, unless sooner removed. And the Governor, legislative council, and house of representatives, shall have authority to make laws in all cases for the good government of the district, not repugnant to the principles and Articles in this Ordinance established and declared. And all bills having passed by a majority in the house, and by a majority in the council, shall be referred to the Governor for his assent; but no bill or legislative Act whatever, shall be of any force without his assent. The Governor shall have power to convene, prorogue and dissolve the General Assembly, when in his opinion it shall be expedient.

The Governor, Judges, legislative Council, Secretary, and such other Officers as Congress shall appoint in the district shall take an Oath or Affirmation of fidelity, and of Office, the Governor before the president of Congress, and all other Officers before the Governor. As soon as a legislature shall be formed in the district, the Council and house assembled in one room, shall have authority by joint ballot to elect a Delegate to Congress, who shall have a seat in Congress, with a right of debating, but not of voting, during this temporary Government.

And for extending the fundamental principles of civil and religious liberty, which form the basis whereon these republics, their laws and constitutions are erected; to fix and establish those principles as the basis of all laws, constitutions and governments, which forever hereafter shall be formed in the said territory; to provide also for the establishment of States and permanent government therein, and for their admission to a share in the federal Councils on an equal footing with the original States, at as early periods as may be consistent with the general interest,

It is hereby Ordained and declared by the authority aforesaid, That the following Articles shall be considered as Articles of compact between the Original States and the people and States in the said territory, and forever remain unalterable, unless by common consent, *to wit*,

Article the First. No person demeaning himself in a peaceable and orderly manner shall ever be molested on account of his mode of worship or religious sentiments in the said territory.

Article the Second. The Inhabitants of the said territory shall always be entitled to the benefits of the writ of habeas corpus, and of the trial by Jury; of a proportionate representation of the people in the legislature, and of judicial proceedings according to the course of the common law; all persons shall be bailable unless for capital offences, where the proof shall be evident, or the presumption great; all fines shall be moderate, and no cruel or unusual punishments shall be inflicted; no man shall be deprived of his liberty or property but by the judgment of his peers, or the law of the land; and should the public exigencies make it necessary for the common preservation to take any persons property, or to demand his particular services, full compensation shall be made for the same; and in the just preservation of rights and property it is understood and declared; that no law ought ever to be made, or have force in the said territory, that shall in any manner whatever interfere with, or affect private contracts or engagements, bona fide and without fraud previously formed.

Article the Third. Religion, Morality <u>and knowledge being necessary to good government and the happiness of mankind</u>, Schools and the means of education shall forever be encouraged. The utmost good faith shall always be observed toward the Indians, their lands and property shall never be taken from them without their consent; and in their property, rights and liberty, they never shall be invaded or disturbed, unless in just and lawful wars authorised by Congress; but laws founded in justice and humanity shall from time to time be made, for preventing wrongs being done to them, and for preserving peace and friendship with them.

Article the Fourth. The said territory, and the States which may be formed therein shall forever remain a part of this Confederacy of the United States of America, subject to the Articles of Confederation, and to such alterations therein as shall be constitutionally made; and to all the Acts and Ordinances of the United States in Congress Assembled, conformable thereto. The Inhabitants and Settlers in the said territory, shall be subject to pay a part of the federal debts contracted or to be contracted, and a proportional part of the expences of Government, to be apportioned on them by Congress, according to the same common rule and measure by which apportionments thereof shall be made on the other States; and the taxes for paying their proportion, shall be laid and levied by the authority and direction of the legislatures of the district or districts or new States, as in the original States, within the time agreed upon by the United States in Congress Assembled. The Legislatures of those districts, or new States, shall never interfere with the primary disposal of the Soil by the United States in Congress Assembled, nor with any regulations Congress may find necessary for securing the title in such soil to the bona fide purchasers. No tax shall be imposed on lands the property of the United States; and in no case shall non resident proprietors be taxed higher than residents. The navigable Waters leading into the Mississippi and St. Lawrence, and the carrying places between the same shall be common highways, and forever free, as well to the Inhabitants of the said territory, as to the Citizens of the United States, and those of any other States that may be admitted into the Confederacy, without any tax, impost or duty therefor.

Article the Fifth. There shall be formed in the said territory, not less than three nor more than five States, and the boundaries of the States, as soon as Virginia shall alter her act of cession and consent to the same, shall become fixed and established as follows, to wit: The Western State in the said territory, shall be bounded by the Mississippi, the Ohio and Wabash rivers; a direct line drawn from the Wabash and post Vincents due North to the territorial line between the United States and Canada, and by the said territorial line to the lake of the Woods and Mississippi. The middle State shall be bounded by the said direct line, the Wabash from post Vincents to the Ohio; by the Ohio, by direct line drawn due North from the mouth of the great Miami to the said territorial line, and by the said territorial line. The eastern State shall be bounded by the last mentioned direct line, the Ohio, Pennsylvania, and the said territorial line; provided however, and it is further understood and declared, that the boundaries of these three States, shall be subject so far to be altered, that if Congress shall hereafter find it expedient, they shall have authority to form one or two States in that part of the said territory which lies north of an east and west line drawn through the southerly bend or extreme of lake Michigan; and whenever any of the said States shall have sixty thousand free Inhabitants therein, such State shall be admitted by its Delegates into the Congress of the United States, on an equal footing with the original States, in all respects whatever; and shall be at liberty to form a permanent

constitution and State government, provided the constitution and government so to be formed, shall be
republican, and in conformity to the principles contained in these Articles; and so far as it can be consistent with the general interest of the Confederacy, such
admission shall be allowed at an earlier period, and
when there may be a less number of free Inhabitants in
the State than sixty thousand.

Article the Sixth. There shall be neither Slavery nor
involuntary Servitude in the said territory otherwise
than in the punishment of crimes, whereof the party
shall have been duly convicted; provided always that
any person escaping into the same, from whom labor or
service is lawfully claimed in any one of the original
States, such fugitive may be lawfully reclaimed and
conveyed to the person claiming his or her labor or
service as aforesaid.

Be it Ordained by the Authority aforesaid, that the
Resolutions of the 23d of April 1784 relative to the
subject of this ordinance be, and the same are hereby
repealed and declared null and void.

Select Bibliography

The Harvard Guide to American History is an indispensable volume of primary and secondary sources. For printed public documents pertaining to the Old Northwest, see especially pages 67–87 in the one-volume, revised edition, Frank Freidel, ed. (Cambridge and London: The Belknap Press of Harvard University Press: 1974). Many of the sources listed below contain bibliographies to which students of the Old Northwest should refer.

Abernethy, Thomas P. *Western Lands and the American Revolution.* New York, 1937.

Adams, J. Q., ed. "The Diaries of the Rev. Seth Williston, D.D., 1796–1800." *Journal of the Presbyterian Historical Society.* Vols. 9 and 10 (1917–1918, 1919–1920).

Adams, Willi Paul. *The First American Constitutions:Republican Ideology and the Making of the State Constitutions in the Revolutionary Era.* Chapel Hill, N.C., 1980.

Alvord, Clarence W., ed. *Cahokia Records, 1778–1790.* Springfield, Ill., 1907.

————. *The Illinois Country, 1673–1818.* Springfield, Ill., 1920.

————, ed. *Kalkaskia Records, 1778–1790.* Springfield, Ill., 1909.

American State Papers: Documents, Legislative and Executive. 38 vols. 1832–1861. These volumes cover the first twenty-five congresses, 1789–1838.

Badger, Joseph. *A Memoir of Rev. Joseph Badger; Containing an Autobiography, and Selections from His Private Journal and Correspondence.* Hudson, Ohio, 1851.

Bailyn, Bernard. *The Ideological Origins of the American Revolution.* Cambridge, Mass., 1967.

————. *Voyagers to the West: A Passage in the Peopling of America on the Eve of the Revolution.* New York, 1986.

Ballagh, James C., ed. *The Letters of Richard Henry Lee.* 2 vols. New York, 1911–1914.

Bancroft, George. *History of the United States of America, From the Discovery of the Continent.* 6 vols. New York, 1883–1885.

Banner, Lois W. "The Protestant Crusade: Religious Missions, Benevolence, and Reform in the United States." Ph.D. diss., Columbia University, 1970.

————. "Religious Benevolence as Social Control: A Critique of an Interpretation." *Journal of American History* 60 (June 1973): 23–41.

Barnhart, John D. *Valley of Democracy: The Frontier Versus the Plantation in the Ohio Valley, 1775–1818.* Bloomington, Ind., 1953.

Barrett, Jay A. *Evolution of the Ordinance of 1787, with an Account of the Earlier Plans for the Government of the Northwest Territory.* New York, 1891.

Basler, Roy P., ed. *The Collected Works of Abraham Lincoln.* 9 vols. New Brunswick, N.J., 1953–1955.

Berkhofer, Robert F., Jr."Jefferson, the Ordinance of 1784, and the Origins of the American Territorial System." *William and Mary Quarterly* 3d ser., 29 (April 1972): 231–62.

Berwanger, Eugene H. *The Frontier Against Slavery: Western Anti-Negro Prejudice and the Slavery Extension Controversy.* Urbana, Ill., 1967.

Billington, Ray Allen. "The Historians of the Northwest Ordinance." *Journal of the Illinois State Historical Society* 40 (December 1947): 397–413.

————. *Westward Expansion: A History of the American Frontier.* 3d ed. New York, 1967.

Bloch, Ruth H. *Visionary Republic: Millennial Themes in American Thought, 1756–1800.* New York, 1985.

Bloom, John Porter, ed. *The American Territorial System.* Athens, Ohio, 1973.

————. "The Continental Nation: Our Trinity of Revolutionary Testaments." *Western Historical Quarterly* 6 (January 1975): 5–15.

Bodo, John R. *The Protestant Clergy and Public Issues, 1812–1848.* Princeton, 1954.

Boggess, Arthur C. *The Settlement of Illinois, 1778–1830.* Freeport, N.Y., 1970, reprint of 1908 ed.

Bogue, Allan G., et al., eds. *The West of the American People.* Itasca, Ill., 1970.

Bond, Beverley W. *The Civilization of the Old Northwest.* New York, 1934.

Boorstin, Daniel J. *The Americans: The Colonial Experience.* New York, 1958.

Bourne, Kenneth. *Britain and the Balance of Power in North America, 1815–1908.* Berkeley, 1967.

Boyd, Julian P., et al., eds. *The Papers of Thomas Jefferson.* 20 vols.

Princeton, 1950–1982. Vol. 21 is an index, Charles T. Cullen, et al., eds. Princeton, 1983.

Bray, Thomas W. *A Dissertation on the Sixth Vial.* Hartford, 1780.

Bridges, Roger D., ed. "John Mason Peck on Illinois Slavery." *Journal of the Illinois State Historical Society* 75 (Autumn 1982): 179–217.

Brown, Richard M. *The South Carolina Regulators.* Cambridge, Mass., 1963.

Buell, Rowena, ed. *The Memoirs of Rufus Putnam.* Cambridge, Mass., 1903.

Burke, Colin B. *American Collegiate Populations: A Test of the Traditional View.* New York, 1982.

Burnet, Jacob. *Notes on the Early Settlement of the North-Western Territory.* Cincinnati, 1847.

Burnett, Edmund C. *The Continental Congress* New York, 1941.

———, ed. *Letters of Members of the Continental Congress.* 8 vols. Washington, D.C., 1921–1936.

Burnett, Howard R. "Early History of Vincennes University." *Indiana Magazine of History* 29 (June 1933): 114–21.

Burt, A. L. *The United States, Great Britain, and British North America, 1783–1815.* New Haven, 1940.

Carter, Clarence E. and John Porter Bloom, eds. *The Territorial Papers of the United States.* 27 vols. Washington, D.C., 1934.

Caruso, John Anthony. *The Great Lakes Frontier.* New York, 1961.

Chase, Salmon P. *The Address and Reply on the Presentation of a Testimonial to S. P. Chase, by the Colored People of Cincinnati.* Cincinnati, 1845.

———. *Reclamation of Fugitives From Justice. An Argument for the Defendant, Submitted to the Supreme Court of the United States at the December Term, 1846, in the Case of Wharton Jones vs. John Van Zandt.* Cincinnati, 1847.

———. *Speech of Salmon P. Chase, in the Case of the Colored Woman, Matilda, Who Was Brought Before Court of Common Pleas of Hamilton County, Ohio, by Writ of Habeas Corpus, March 11, 1837.* Cincinnati, 1837.

———, ed. *The Statutes of Ohio and the Northwestern Territory.* 3 vols. Cincinnati, 1833–1835.

Clark, Thomas D., *Indiana University: Midwestern Pioneer,* 4 vols. (Bloomington, 1970–1977).

Cohen, William. "Thomas Jefferson and the Problem of Slavery." *Journal of American History* 56 (December 1969): 503–26.

Coles, Edward. *History of the Ordinance of 1787.* Philadelphia, 1856.

Congregational Church in Connecticut. *Address to the Inhabitants of the New Settlements in the Northern and Western Parts of the United States.* New Haven, 1793.

————. *An Address of the General Association of Connecticut, to the District Associations.* Norwich, Conn., 1797.

————. *A Continuation of the Narrative of the Missions.* New Haven, 1797.

Connecticut Evangelical Magazine 1–6 (1800–1805).

Craig, Gerald M. *Upper Canada: The Formative Years, 1784–1841.* Toronto, 1963.

Cram, Jacob. *Journal of a Missionary Tour.* Rochester, N.Y., 1809.

Cremin, Lawrence A. *American Education: The Colonial Experience, 1607–1783.* New York, 1970.

————. *American Education: The National Experience, 1783–1876.* New York, 1980.

Curti, Merle and Vernon Carstensen. *The University of Wisconsin: A History, 1848–1925.* 2 vols. Madison, 1949.

Cutler, William Parker and Julia Perkins Cutler. *Life, Journals, and Correspondence of Rev. Manasseh Cutler, LL.D.* 2 vols. Cincinnati, 1888.

Darling, Arthur P. *Our Rising Empire, 1763–1803.* New Haven, 1940.

Debates and Proceedings in the Congress of the United States, 1789–1824. 42 vols. Washington, D.C., 1834–1856.

DePauw, Linda Grant. "Land of the Unfree: Legal Limitations on Liberty in Pre–Revolutionary America." *Maryland Historical Magazine* 68 (Winter 1973): 355–68.

Dexter, Franklin B. *Biographical Sketches of the Graduates of Yale College.* 6 vols. New York, 1885–1912.

————, ed. *The Literary Diary of Ezra Stiles.* 3 vols. New York, 1901.

Donaldson, Thomas. *The Public Domain.* Washington, D.C., 1884.

Downes, Randolph C. *Council Fires on the Upper Ohio.* Pittsburgh, 1940.

————. *Frontier Ohio, 1788–1803.* Columbus, 1935.

Dunbar, Willis F. *The Michigan Record in Higher Education.* Detroit, 1963.

Dunn, Jacob P. "Slavery Petitions and Papers." *Indiana Historical Society Publication* 2 (Indianapolis, 1894): 443–529.

Dwight, Timothy. *The Duty of Americans, at the Present Crisis.* New Haven, 1798.

Eblen, Jack E. *The First and Second United States Empires: Governors and Territorial Government, 1784–1912.* Pittsburgh, 1968.

————. "Origins of the United States Colonial System: The Ordinance of 1787." *Wisconsin Magazine of History* 51 (Summer 1968): 294–314.

Ekirch, A. Roger, Jr. *"Poor Carolina": Politics and Society in Colonial North Carolina, 1729–1776.* Chapel Hill, 1981.

Elliot, Jonathan, ed. *Debates in the Several State Conventions on the Adoption of the Federal Constitution.* 2d ed., 5 vols. Philadelphia, 1888.

Elsbree, Oliver Wendell. *The Rise of the Missionary Spirit.* Williamsport, Penn., 1928.

Emmons, Nathaneal. *A Sermon, Delivered Before the Massachusetts Missionary Society . . . May 27, 1800.* Charlestown, Mass., 1800.

Farrand, Max. *The Framing of the Constitution of the United States.* New Haven, 1913.

———. ed. *The Records of the Federal Convention of 1787.* 2d rev. ed., 4 vols. New Haven, 1987.

Fehrenbacher, Don. *The Dred Scott Case.* New York, 1978.

Finkelman, Paul. *An Imperfect Union: Slavery, Federalism, and Comity.* Chapel Hill, 1981.

———. "Slavery and the Northwest Ordinance: A Study in Ambiguity." *Journal of the Early Republic* 6 (Winter 1986): 343–70.

Fitzpatrick, John C., ed. *The Writings of George Washington.* 39 vols. Washington, D.C. 1931–1944.

Ford, W. C., et al., eds. *Journals of the Continental Congress, 1774–1789.* 34 vols. Washington, D.C., 1904–1937.

Foster, Charles I. *An Errand of Mercy: The Evangelical United Front, 1790–1837.* Chapel Hill, 1960.

Galbreath, Charles B. "The Ordinance of 1787: Its Origin and Authorship." *Ohio Archaeological and Historical Quarterly* 33 (April 1924): 111–75.

Gates, Paul and Robert W. Swenson. *History of Public Land Law Development.* Washington, D.C., 1968.

Gillet, Alexander. "True Christianity the Safety of this World." In *Sermons on Important Subjects.* Hartford, Conn., 1797.

Glover, Wilbur H. "The Agricultural College Crisis of 1885." *Wisconsin Magazine of History* 32 (September 1948): 17–25.

———. *Farm and College: The College of Agriculture of the University of Wisconsin.* Madison, 1952.

Good, Harry G. and James D. Teller. *A History of American Education.* New York, 1973.

Goodykoontz, Colin B. *Home Missions on the American Frontier.* Caldwell, Idaho, 1939.

Griffin, Clifford S. *Their Brothers' Keepers: Moral Stewardship in the United States, 1800–1865.* New Brunswick, N.J., 1960.

Griffin, J. David. "Historians and the Sixth Article of the Ordinance of 1787." *Ohio History* 78 (Autumn 1969): 252–60.

Harris, N. Dwight. *The History of Negro Servitude in Illinois.* Chicago, 1904.

Hart, Levi. *Religious Improvements of the Death of Great Men.* Norwich, Conn., 1800.

Havighurst, Walter. *The Miami Years, 1809–1969.* New York, 1969.

Hepburn, William Murray and Louis Martin Sears. *Purdue University: Fifty Years of Progress.* Indianapolis, 1925.

Herbst, Jurgen. *From Crisis to Crisis: American College Government, 1636–1819.* Cambridge, Mass., 1982.

Hubbard, Benjamin H. *A History of Public Land Policies.* New York, 1924, reprinted 1939.

Hinsdale, Burke A. *The Old Northwest: With a View of the Thirteen Colonies as Constituted by the Royal Charters.* New York, 1888.

Hooker, Richard J., ed. *The Carolina Backcountry on the Eve of the Revolution; The Journal and Other Writings of Charles Woodmason, Anglican Itinerant.* Chapel Hill, 1953.

Hoover, Thomas N. *The History of Ohio University.* Athens, Ohio, 1954.

Horsman, Reginald. *Expansion and American Indian Policy.* East Lansing, Mich., 1969.

Hulbert, Archer B. *Ohio in the Time of the Confederation.* Marietta, Ohio, 1918.

————, ed. *The Records and Original Proceedings of the Ohio Company.* 2 vols. Marietta, Ohio, 1917.

Isbell, Egbert R. *A History of Eastern Michigan University, 1849–1965.* Ypsilanti, Mich., 1971.

Jensen, Merrill. *The Articles of Confederation: An Interpretation of the Social–Constitutional History of the American Republic, 1774–1781.* Madison, Wis., 1940.

————. "The Cession of the Old Northwest." *Mississippi Valley Historical Review* 23 (June 1936): 27–48.

————, ed. *Constitutional Documents and Records, 1776–1787.* Madison, Wis., 1976.

————. "The Creation of the National Domain, 1781–1784." *Mississippi Valley Historical Review* 26 (December 1939): 323–42.

————. *The New Nation: A History of the United States During the Confederation, 1781–1789.* New York, 1950.

Keller, Charles Roy. *The Second Great Awakening in Connecticut.* New Haven, 1942.

Kennedy, William S. *The Plan of Union: Or a History of the Presbyterian and Congregational Churches of the Western Reserve.* Hudson, Ohio, 1856.

Kersey, Harry A., Jr., *John Milton Gregory and the University of Illinois.* Urbana, Ill., 1968.

King, Charles R., ed. *The Life and Correspondence of Rufus King. . .* 6 vols. New York, 1894–1900.

Kinnison, William A. *Building Sullivant's Pyramid: An Administrative History of the Ohio State University, 1870–1907.* Columbus, 1970.

Kuhn, Madison. *Michigan State: The First Hundred Years, 1855–1955.* East Lansing, Mich., 1955.

Kurtz, Stephen G. and James H. Hutson, eds. *Essays on the American Revolution*. Chapel Hill, 1973.

Lee, Chauncy. *The Tree of Knowledge of Political Good and Evil*. Bennington, Vt., 1800.

Lindley, Harlow, et al. *History of the Ordinance of 1787 and the Old Northwest Territory*. Marietta, Ohio, 1937.

Ludlum, David M. *Social Ferment in Vermont, 1791–1850*. New York, 1939.

Lyman, William. *The Happy Nation*. Hartford, Conn., 1806.

Lynd, Staughton, ed. *Class Conflict, Slavery and the United States Constitution*. Indianapolis, 1967.

McColley, Robert. *Slavery and Jeffersonian Virginia*. 2d ed. Urbana, Ill., 1973.

McDonald, Forrest and Ellen Shapiro McDonald. *Confederation and Constitution, 1781–1789*. New York, 1968.

McLaughlin, Andrew C. *The Confederation and the Constitution, 1783–1789*. New York and London, 1905.

Malloy, William M., et al., eds. *Treaties, Conventions, International Acts, Protocols, and Agreements Between the United States and Other Powers, 1776–1937*. 4 vols. Washington, D.C., 1910–1938.

Manning, William R., ed. *Diplomatic Correspondence of the United States. Canadian Relations, 1784–1860*. 4 vols. Washington, D.C., 1940.

Marshall, Helen E. *Grandest of Enterprises: Illinois State Normal University, 1857–1957*. Normal, Ill., 1956.

Massachusetts Baptist Missionary Magazine.

Massachusetts Missionary Magazine.

Mathews, Lois Kimball. *The Expansion of New England*. Boston, 1909.

Newcomer, Lee Nathaniel. "Manasseh Cutler's Writings: A Note on Editorial Practice." *Mississippi Valley Historical Review* 47 (June 1960): 88–101.

Miller, Edward Alanson. *The History of Educational Legislation in Ohio from 1803 to 1850*. New York, 1969.

Mills, Samuel J. and Daniel Smith. *Report of a Missionary Tour through that Part of the United States which Lies West of the Allegheny Mountains*. Andover, Mass., 1815.

Missionary Society of Connecticut. *An Act to Incorporate the Trustees*. Hartford, 1803.

————. *Address from the Trustees . . . to the Ministers and People*. Hartford, 1807.

————. *Address to the People of Connecticut*. Hartford, 1801.

————. *The Constitution of the Missionary Society of Connecticut*. Hartford, 1800.

————. *Interesting Account of Religion in France*. New York, 1803.

————. A Narrative on the Subject of Missions. Hartford, 1793–1810.

————. A Second Address from the Trustees of the Missionary Society . . . and a Narrative on the Subject of Missions. Hartford, 1802.

————. A Summary of Christian Doctrine and Practice: Designed Especially for the Use of People in the New Settlements. Hartford, 1804.

Moore, Glover. The Missouri Controversy, 1819–1821. Lexington, Ky., 1953.

Morgan, Edmund S. The Birth of the Republic, 1763–1789. Chicago, 1956.

————. The Meaning of Independence. New York, 1978.

Morris, Richard B. The Forging of the Union, 1781–1789. New York, 1987.

————, ed. Basic Documents on the Confederation and Constitution. New York, 1970.

Nevins, Allan. The American States During and After the Revolution, 1775–1789. New York, 1924.

Onuf, Peter S. "From Constitution to Higher Law:The Reinterpretation of the Northwest Ordinance." Ohio History (Winter–Spring 1985): 5–33.

————. "Liberty, Development, and Union: Visions of the West in the 1780s." William and Mary Quarterly, ser 3, 43 (April 1986): 179–213.

————. The Origins of the Federal Republic: Jurisdictional Controversies in the United States, 1775–1787. Philadelphia, 1983.

Palmer, Edwin Pond. Historical Discourse in Commemoration of the One Hundredth Anniversary of the Missionary Society of Connecticut. Hartford, 1929.

Pease, Theodore C. "The Ordinance of 1787." Mississippi Valley Historical Review 25 (September 1938): 167–80.

Peckham, Howard H. The Making of the University of Michigan, 1817–1967. Ann Arbor, 1967.

Perkins, Nathan, ed. A Narrative of a Tour through the State of Vermont from April 27 to June 12, 1789. Woodstock, Vt., 1937.

Peters, William E. Legal History of the Ohio University. Cincinnati, 1910.

Peterson, Merrill D. Thomas Jefferson and the New Nation: A Biography. New York, 1970.

Philbrick, Francis S., ed. Laws of the Indiana Territory, 1801–1809. Springfield, Ill., 1930.

————. The Rise of the West, 1754–1830. New York, 1965.

Poole, William Frederick. The Ordinance of 1787, and Dr. Manasseh Cutler as an Agent in its Formation. Cambridge, Mass., 1876.

Price, Richard Rees. The Financial Support of State Universities. Cambridge, Mass., 1924.

Purcell, Richard J. *Connecticut in Transition.* Washington, D.C., 1918.

Quaife, Milo M. "The Significance of the Ordinance of 1787." *Journal of the Illinois State Historical Society* 30 (January 1938): 415–28.

Rainsford, George N. *Congress and Higher Education in the Nineteenth Century.* Knoxville, Tenn., 1972.

Rakove, Jack N. *The Beginnings of National Politics: An Interpretive History of the Continental Congress.* New York, 1979.

Robbins, Ammi Ruhamah. *The Empires and Dominions of the World.* Hartford, 1789.

Robbins, Roy M. *Our Landed Heritage: The Public Domain, 1776–1936.* Princeton, 1942.

Robbins, Thomas. *The Diary of Thomas Robbins, D.D., 1796–1854.* 2 vols. Boston, 1886–1887.

Robinson, Donald. *Slavery in the Structure of American Politics, 1765– 1820.* New York, 1971.

Rohrbough, Malcolm J. *The Trans-Appalachian Frontier, 1775–1850.* New York, 1978.

Roosevelt, Theodore. *The Winning of the West.* 6 vols. New York, 1889.

Rossiter, Clinton. *1787: Grand Convention.* New York, 1966.

Rudolph, Frederick, ed. *Essays on Education in the Early Republic.* Cambridge, Mass., 1965.

Rutland, Robert A. *The Ordeal of the Constitution: The Antifederalists and the Ratification Struggle of 1787–1788.* Norman, Okla., 1966.

Schermerhorn, John F. and Samuel J. Mills. *A Correct View of That Part of the United States Which Lies West of the Allegheny Mountains.* Hartford, 1814.

Scott, Donald M. *From Office to Profession: The New England Ministry, 1750–1850.* Philadelphia, 1978.

Shriver, Phillip R. "America's Other Bicentennial." *The Old Northwest: A Journal of Regional Life and Letters* 9 (Fall 1983): 219–35.

Smith, William Henry. *The St. Claire Papers: The Life and Public Services of Arthur St. Claire.* 2 vols. Cincinnati, 1882.

Solberg, Winton. *The University of Illinois, 1867–1894: An Intellectual and Cultural History.* Urbana, 1968.

Solomon, Barbara M., ed. *Travels in New England and New York.* 4 vols. Cambridge, Mass., 1969.

Sprague, William B., ed. *Annals of the American Pulpit.* 9 vols. New York, 1857–1869.

Stagg, J. C. A. *Mr. Madison's War: Politics, Diplomacy and Warfare in the Early American Republic, 1783–1830.* Princeton, 1983.

Stewart, Gordon T. *The Origins of Canadian Politics.* Vancouver, 1986.

Stewart, Gordon T. and G. A. Rawlyk. *The Nova Scotia Yankees and the American Revolution*. Toronto, 1972.

Stiles, Ezra. *The United States Elevated to Glory and Honour*. New Haven, 1783.

Stone, Albert E., ed. *Letters from an American Farmer and Sketches of Eighteenth-Century America by J. Hector St. John de Crevecoeur*. New York: Penguin, 1981.

Stone, Frederick D. "The Ordinance of 1787." *The Pennsylvania Magazine of History and Biography* 13 (1889).

Strong, Cyprian. *Connecticut Election Sermon, May 9, 1799*. Hartford, 1799.

Sweet, William Warren. *Religion on the American Frontier*. 4 vols. Chicago, 1931–1939.

Taylor, Howard Cromwell. *The Educational Significance of the Early Federal Land Ordinances*. New York, 1922.

Thornbrough, Emma Lou. *The Negro in Indiana*. Indianapolis, 1957.

Thorpe, Francis Newton, ed. *The Federal and State Constitutions, Colonial Charters, and Other Organic Laws of States, Territories and Colonies Now or Heretofore Forming the United States of America*. 7 vols. Washington, D.C., 1909.

Turner, Frederick Jackson. *The Frontier in American History*. New York, 1920.

United States Statutes at Large. . ., 1874–.

Wiecek, William M. *The Sources of Antislavery Constitutionalism in America, 1760–1848*. Ithaca, N.Y., 1977.

Wilson, Charles Jay. "The Negro in Early Ohio." *Ohio Archaeological and Historical Publications* 39 (1930).

Wood, Gordon S. *The Creation of the American Republic, 1776–1787*. Chapel Hill, 1969.

Zilversmit, Arthur. *The First Emancipation*. Chicago, 1967.

Index